The Science of Rapid Skill Acquisition:
Advanced Methods for Learn, Remember, and Master New Skills and Information

By Peter Hollins,
Author and Researcher at
petehollins.com

Table of Contents

The Science of Rapid Skill Acquisition:
Advanced Methods for Learn, Remember, and Master New Skills and Information 3

Table of Contents 5

Chapter 1. Learn with Rapid Skill Acquisition 7
    What to Learn? 14
    Stages of Learning 20

Chapter 2. Strategic Planning 29
    Under Deconstruction 30
    Mix Styles and Mediums 36
    Gather Information and Resources 55

Chapter 3. It's Just Practice 69
    Deliberate Practice 71
    Interleaved Practice 78
    Spaced Repetition 84
    Problem-Based Learning 94
    "When you lose, don't lose the lesson." 107
    Prioritize It - obviously! 116

Chapter 4. Deep Comprehension 127
    Elaborative Interrogation 128
    The Feynman Technique 136

    Bloom's Taxonomy 142
    The Curiosity Muscle 153

Chapter 5. Stack Your Skills 165

Chapter 6. Social and Physical Surroundings 183
    No Negative Nancys 187
    Role Models, Support Systems, and Hotbeds 192
    Physical Surroundings 206

Chapter 7. Manage Your Expectations 217
    Remain Realistic 218
    What's The Toll? 226
    Constant Confusion 231
    You Know Nothing 234

Summary Guide 241

Chapter 1. Learn with Rapid Skill Acquisition

Like many children, I was forced to play an instrument in my youth. My parents gave me the choice between piano, saxophone, and violin. However, there was already a piano in our household despite the fact that no one else in my family played. It seemed that they had a strong preference, and weren't really presenting me with a real choice. I took the hint and signed up for piano lessons starting the next week.

I never really excelled at piano, despite playing for seven years overall. Some kids can get to Carnegie Hall in that time span.

And wasn't Mozart composing concertos when he was only four or five years old? I was playing relatively simple songs for the vast majority of those seven years. It wasn't necessarily a waste of money, but I was no standout. I was average.

Was it just due to a simple lack of talent on my part? Maybe, but in hindsight probably not.

Talent may have been involved to some extent, but as far as I can remember, my practice and rehearsal time was severely lacking. It was also punctuated by an intense lack of patience on my part because most of my other friends had new mountain bikes that year and I was stuck inside, plunking on the piano during the beautiful summer months of carefree biking. I didn't want to be in front of the piano, and I didn't focus when I was.

On the other hand, I had a friend from school who started playing piano at around the same time as me. We commiserated constantly, but I soon grew jealous of him as he progressed far more quickly than me in his piano skills. In terms of *piano levels*, he was able to advance every year while my teacher didn't even attempt to advance me each year—I was up every other year at best. We used to perform at the same recitals, but this suddenly stopped during our second year. He had been promoted to the advanced student recitals, while I was still in the land of the beginners.

I didn't have the foresight at the time to ask what he was doing differently, but talent notwithstanding, it's clear that he was far more regimented in practice, rehearsal, and discipline. After all, I was familiar with his mother, and I knew she was fairly strict and severe. I also heard she was formerly a collegiate tennis player and could hit quite hard with a wooden backscratcher (this part is true).

What does it take to learn something optimally and in the shortest time possible? Again, talent may contribute. The willingness to put your head down, embrace the work, and persist until your struggles yield something—that surely determines an important portion of how you learn. You can get by with just those two ingredients in the beginning, but there are more effective and efficient ways to learn new skills in whatever circumstance you find yourself in.

Learning new things is something we associate more with our passions or hobbies: knitting, swimming, tennis, or an instrument. But it has the capacity to affect your life in much greater ways. In fact, learning new skills represents the ability to change your life and circumstances from top to bottom. Understanding how to accelerate this process for yourself just means that you can change your life even more quickly in the direction that you want.

Rapid skill acquisition, despite my early history with piano, has been key throughout my academic and work careers. I believe it has the potential to affect you similarly, so dig in and get ready to start *learning how to learn*.

We live in a time when we can learn things faster than ever before in history.

Information on almost any topic we want to investigate is almost instantly accessible. Cheap or even free tutorials exist online for any skill or expertise we want to attain. It's never been easier for an individual to take an interest, build a level of expertise, and even gain certification for completing a field of study, all in the privacy of their own living rooms. If you didn't know a certain fact even 20 years ago, you would have to trek to a library and flip through an encyclopedia for hours just to find your answer. Who can be bothered with that?

All the tools are there for us now, and they're accessible and easy to use. Right now, we can shape our lives by acquiring new abilities more than any generation in the history of the world.

So why don't we?

Is it because we haven't learned enough about how to *learn*? If so, it's not really our fault (though it does end up being our problem to deal with).

When we first experienced learning, it was in one form only: passively. This is pretty much what you'll receive in traditional school settings. Information is presented, you take it in, and you repeat it again at some certain point. In certain classes, we were expected to more or less memorize and regurgitate information, which isn't necessarily to the best way to retain it for future use. School was seen as something to just get through, and for some of us that meant spending as little mental effort as we could get away with. True learning and synthesis was not the goal, and thus we don't really know how to work toward that.

When you want to learn something new on your own, you just might realize that you have no idea where to start, and your years of learning how to regurgitate aren't doing you any good.

It's hard to utilize information that you only know to repeat—you weren't taught how to turn it into anything practical, or taught which parts of what you learned were most important. We certainly weren't taught how to process and direct what we learned either: how to take notes, manage time, focus intensely, or set priorities. Information for information's sake isn't very valuable. Besides, much of what we learned in school is already outdated thanks to changing technology and the general advancement of time.

There really is no other option besides learning for someone who wants to change their circumstances. If you can't learn effectively, then you're never going to move forward. Especially in these times when self-learning is so convenient, you're missing out on an essential skill to determining your own life.

Take a friend of mine, for instance. She went through a divorce, and after 10 years of marriage she'd never had a job and didn't have any marketable skills. But she taught herself how to make jewelry step by step; she didn't attend a class because she couldn't afford it. After five years of practice she was able to launch a custom-made jewelry business, and she still runs it out of her own home—which she was able to purchase only three years later. She was able to seize upon an interest of hers, find resources, and alter the course of her life. It certainly wasn't from regurgitating information that her craft improved!

The psychology of setting your own path, rather than just following someone else's curriculum, is a bonus almost from the start. Activating your self-will, taking ownership, and becoming wholly engaged are necessary elements to self-learning, and you'll find they are elements that translate to how satisfying your life is.

Learning a new skill in particular can increase the overall value of your life, regardless of your age, background, upbringing, or position. The sense of accomplishment is a reward in itself, but you can also improve your status quo or employment situation, fulfill your personal ambitions, enhance your all-around abilities, and even open the door to new abilities you might want to learn.

What to Learn?

Those of us wanting to learn a new trade or skill and alter the course of our lives have no lack of options. Opportunities are always abound, no matter how it seems. It can be a taxing job to decide what you really want to devote your time to, especially if you're choosing to do it on your own and not being told by someone else—maybe for the first time in your life!

How do you decide what to concentrate on?

Now, this is a question that isn't always so important. Sometimes we want to learn new knowledge or a skill just because we want to. That's learning for learning's sake, and it doesn't necessarily have to lead anywhere. But for those of us that want to optimize our time and mental bandwidth...

As a thought exercise, think about all the skills you would want to learn, either for recreational or professional purposes. Don't be surprised if you come up with a double-digit number of them; I'm sure you could come up with 10, 15, or even more. Obviously, you won't be able to conquer all of them at once. None of us have an unlimited amount of time, so we need to pinpoint a small number of skills that we can handle or matter the most.

Most likely you could cover two or three at most in a given time period, between what you learn for both your work and your leisure time. A few things can factor into your decision.

Purpose. What's the driving reason you want to build this new skill? Is it to bring in more money, to gain a new hobby, enhance your relationship, improve your physical or mental health? Determine the goal that's most important to you, and learn skills that will build toward it. You might be starting a new business but have to learn basic accounting. You might be wanting more adventure, so decided to learn mountain-climbing. You might be traveling abroad in the future and want to learn a new language. Understanding the greater purpose behind the pain is important, because you will know that the hard work will lead to a worthwhile payoff.

Supply and demand. This is for skills that specifically relate to job and career, and some skills are more marketable than others. They're abilities for which there's an acute need but low supply. You can find a lot of coders who can type out HTML or CSS code in their sleep—but far fewer who understand Ruby on Rails, Python, C#, or even JavaScript (as is my understanding as a non-coder). Whenever possible, select a skill that can boost your bankability. If it's not money you're after, then find the skill that has the most value to you in another sense (if you love Mexican food, then learn how to make that—don't worry about mastering French cuisine).

Talent. If you have an innate predisposition, that can be a difference-maker in choosing a certain skill. Capitalize on your natural talent and you'll be more effective and able to advance in learning your skill more quickly. A common frustration in employment is toiling away at a task that doesn't use any of our best abilities. Everyone is endowed with a certain talent that's easier for them to execute than others. Which new skill will you be able to master more swiftly because it takes advantage of your natural abilities?

The simple truth is that it's far more satisfying, profitable, and freeing to be in the top 1% of a skill than the top 10%. It's the 1% who make the most money, who beat the odds to become a professional athlete, and who are always sought-after. Having a natural proclivity can also matter especially if you are low on patience. This is something we'll cover in greater detail later with regard to the concept of skill stacking.

Available opportunities. Look at your current social or work situations. How well do they support the learning of a particular skill? Maybe your company is willing to reimburse you for learning how to master video editing. Maybe you have a friend or family member who's an expert gardener who can mentor you. Maybe there's a low-risk job opening that will pay you as you learn a programming language. What skills does your immediate environment make it easy to acquire?

Related to that, certain skills that are more difficult or complex to achieve will require more tools, attention, time, or money than ones that are simpler. Be honest and pragmatic about which skills are more easily obtainable and affordable given your current set of circumstances. You might want to be an ice sculptor, but that means you'll have to invest in a chainsaw, which is a challenge because you live in an environment where the weather is 90 degrees Fahrenheit year-round. Ceramics or clay work might be more to your wallet's and environment's liking, *for now*.

Life situation. We get hired and fired, we start relationships and break up, we get married and divorced, we get sick, we relocate, we have children—nobody's exempt from sweeping life changes. And some of those transformations will require learning new skills. Your company downsizes and you have to learn how to keep a budget. You become a parent and have to learn how to cook. You're diagnosed with diabetes and have to learn how to exercise. Life situations beget the question "What if?" and make you prepare for them.

When a significant life shift is forced upon you, accept it as much as you can. If it forces you to learn a new life skill, welcome the opportunity. Don't fight or resist the chance, and accept the situation you're currently in. It could be a major force in helping you adapt to your new circumstances.

Stages of Learning

Before we dive into constructing a plan for rapid skill acquisition, it will be helpful to understand what's going to happen when you start on your path to, well, anything. Since most of your education probably took the form of passive learning, as mentioned, you probably aren't aware of how information and knowledge becomes lodged in your head, ready to be applied. Understanding this can lead to a good way to mark progress and anticipate what we're comes next.

In 1970, Noel Burch of Gordon Training International recognized four stages of learning and growing competence everyone goes through when they're learning something new. Let's use the example of learning piano to illustrate these stages (and to reassure my mother that all those years of lessons she spent money on were good for something).

Unconscious incompetence. Simply put, you don't know what you don't know. This stage is when we're first being introduced to a new skill or knowledge—we have no idea what we're doing, what we need to know, or what our objectives are. Inevitably, we'll end up making a lot of errors without even knowing it.

In the piano-learning example, in this stage about the only thing you know is what a piano looks like. You might know what it sounds like. You know something happens when you touch the keys. That's about it. Beyond that, you have no idea how to read music, how your fingers are supposed to move around the keys, or anything about music theory. You might not even know if you're going to pursue it all the way. And you can't play scales yet to save your life.

Conscious incompetence. In the next stage, you know what you don't know but can't do anything about it. The beginning of the middle phase is when you're starting to get acquainted with some of the particulars of the skill you're building. You're aware that there's still plenty you don't know, but you *do* know how to spot those knowledge gaps and how you're going to fill them. You still make mistakes, but now you know you are.

Now you know a few things about the piano. You probably know the notes, and you can probably play some of the scales without too much effort. And you know certain basic points of reading music: what sharps and flats are, what a time signature is, how long you're supposed to hold a note, and maybe a couple of the more basic instructions that tell you to get louder or softer, faster or slower. But you're still learning fingering techniques, still have to go slowly with new pieces, and can't even think about playing anything too complicated. You're not breaking out the Rachmaninoff yet. You know what you need to do, but you can't technically do it because you aren't skilled enough.

Conscious competence. You know what you need to know, and now you can do it. You're starting to get more adept. You're practicing a lot and are able to execute certain aspects of your new skills. You know what you're supposed to do and are making fewer mistakes. But you're not yet a natural at what you're trying to do—you still need to be attentive to your process in order to develop it into a habit.

So you've attained a pretty good proficiency on piano at this point. You have a regular practice schedule. You're learning more intricate parts of music theory. You're able to recognize and play some pieces by ear, although you still have to look up certain chord progressions. There are still levels to go: your fingers' muscle memory is not quite developed enough to play outrageously fast pieces, and most of the time you still need sheet music to play certain songs. But you're very aware that it's starting to pay off.

Unconscious competence. Finally, you know what you know and you can do it without even having to think about it. At last, you've become an expert at the skill. You're extremely proficient, you know every step by heart, you know how to accomplish your goals and adjust seamlessly if needed, and you make few if any errors. As "unconscious" implies, you can practically do this in your sleep—you barely need to think at all when you're doing this new skill because you've totally mastered it.

I'm happy to inform you that you're now quite brilliant on piano. Years of practice have turned your fingers into devices of extraordinary speed. You can play almost anything by ear. The only time you need sheet music is when you're being introduced to a new piece you've never heard before; you memorize it after only a few plays. You almost disappear into the instrument whenever you're playing. You're an expert now. You're playing Carnegie Hall, people are dying to work with you, you're getting Grammy nominations and Elton John is calling you for advice.

Recognizing all these stages whenever we're taking on a new skill is very valuable. It helps set realistic expectations about when and how we're learning and allows us better insight into what we need to do. We can pinpoint where we are and what we're lacking in. We are aiming to get through these four stages *rapidly*.

Most importantly, this process can fend off feelings of disappointment and judgment. By knowing what we're in for, and understanding it's perfectly normal, we feel more encouragement and motivation to press forward. The first stages of learning can be painful, and remember, that's totally normal. Everyone who's mastered a skill has started out not knowing anything. The cure to enduring the first stages is simply to press on.

There's a lot of planning in learning, much of it happening before we even know what we want to do. As with most decisions, we have to qualify what we really need or want and envision the results we're after. Once we've mentally prepared ourselves, psyched ourselves up, and decided to take on the challenge, it's time to start setting our expectations about the skill we're going to acquire.

Takeaways:

- What is learning? Beyond the pain and discomfort and annoyance, learning represents the ability to change your life and circumstances. The problem is, we were never taught how to learn because most of our schooling tended to be passive. Unfortunately, the skill of regurgitating information and filling in the blanks does not serve us well in the real world. What serves us is knowing the most effective methods for learning a skill.

- An important step in learning is to figure out what you want to learn. We have many desires but should only devote our precious time to things that matter. What matters? Things that can increase our happiness and bankability, capitalize on a strength, enhance a life purpose, make the most of an opportunity, or cope with a life circumstance. Not every skill, hobby, or piece of information is created equally, especially in terms of what will create a shift in your life.

- There are four important stages of learning to familiarize yourself with. When you know where you are, you can plan much better the next steps you need to take. The four stages are *unconscious incompetence* (you don't know what you don't know), *conscious incompetence* (you know what you're doing wrong), *conscious competence* (you know how to succeed, but it takes effort and focus), and *unconscious competence* (you can succeed without thinking about it).

Chapter 2. Strategic Planning

Even if you enter into acquiring a new skill with next to no knowledge about it, you can and should try to have some outline in mind about how you're going to learn. A good plan is one that guides you through the new processes but isn't so set in stone that you can't deviate from it if you have to.

It's not everything, but a well-constructed plan is often the difference between success and coming up short. This chapter gives you some strategies and considerations for building a solid project plan for learning a new skill.

Under Deconstruction

One reason some are so apprehensive about learning a new skill is that, from a distance, doing so seems like a huge, daunting undertaking. While that's true in a sense, most of the things we consider skills—cooking, playing music, carpentry, even writing—are more like a collection of smaller-scale skills (we'll call them *subskills*) that work together to form the larger skill.

A solution to taking on a new skill is to break it down into several more workable parts—deconstructing the big job into steps that are skills of their own. The word *deconstruct* automatically makes me think of construction and building a house, which is actually an apt illustration. The skill of building a house doesn't really exist—it is composed of hundreds of subskills, such as electrical engineering, carpentry, planning, drawing blueprints, creative architecture, cement work, tiling, and so on. You'd go crazy if you didn't deconstruct the job.

Deconstruction is taking individual elements, observing what they are and what they do, and understanding how their smaller function fits into the bigger, overall process. Doing so makes self-training and practice far less formidable, as you can concentrate on developing the subskills one by one.

But more than that, not all subskills are created equal. Subskills follow the precept of the famous, universal Pareto principle, also known as "the 80/20 law." This maxim states that 80% of the effects of any given enterprise come from 20% of the causes. The intent of the Pareto principle is to focus on developing that 20% of causes and reducing or eliminating attention to the remaining 80%. For our purposes, that means determining which 20% of subskills are the most crucial to the larger skill and directing your learning to them. That's another reason deconstruction is so important—it's a matter of knowing what to focus on for biggest benefit and progress.

For example, language expert Gabriel Wyner says that when you're beginning to learn a new language, focus only on the 1000 or so most common words in that language first: "After 1,000 words, you'll know 70% of the words in any average text, and 2,000 words provide you with 80% text coverage."

Wyner explains the imbalance even further. Let's say you knew only 10 English words: "the," "(to) be," "of," "and," "a," "to," "in," "he," "have," and "it." If that was the extent of your vocabulary, how much of any text would you recognize?

According to Dr. Paul Nation, the answer is 23.7%. Those 10 words represent 0.00004% of the English language, which has over 250,000 words. But we use those 10 so often that they regularly make up nearly 25% of every sentence we write.

Let's say we eventually increase our vocabulary to a whopping 100 words—including "year," "(to) see," "(to) give," "then," "most," "great," "(to) think," and "there." With that number, Dr. Nation says, we'd have the ability to understand 49% of every sentence uttered.

Let that sink in a bit—with only 100 words, we can recognize nearly half the content of every sentence. Let's be generous and fluff his numbers—that would still mean that with 200 words, we could recognize 40% of the content in each sentence. The fact that *less than one ten-thousandth* of all English words make of almost half of every sentence is kind of a big deal. That is a staggering demonstration of the Pareto principle.

Dr. Alexander Arguelles, another polyglot working in linguistics at the Regional Language Centre of the South East Asian Ministers of Education Organization, breaks it down even further. Arguelles says that every day, the number of words every single speaker of a given language uses is 750. Furthermore, only 2500 words are needed for you to express anything you could possibly want to say. (Although some expressions might be a little awkward or strange, 2500 words are technically all you need.)

That's the Pareto principle in an almost perfect nutshell. To extend it to our lives, take any subject you want to learn and break it down to the tasks that experts in the field have that matter—and those that don't.

Let's think specifically about learning German, a fairly challenging one for native English speakers. A lot of language-learning models start off with the simplest words—"a," "the," "he," "she," and so forth. Then they move to common words and phrases, like "man," "window," "thank you," "library," "apple," and others. Already you can see that the primary focus isn't necessarily on the words you're likely to use every day.

Back up and ask yourself: what are the 300 most commonly used German words beyond what you've learned at the beginning? Lists of them are easy to find on the Internet—find those 300 and break them into even smaller chunks, then practice one chunk at a time.

You can also break down the steps based on your own personal motivations for learning German. Is it for work? Are you planning a trip to Berlin? Do you just want to be able to converse with a German friend? With answers to those questions in mind, you can determine what phrases and concepts you're more likely to use than other people learning the language—figure out those words as well and treat them in the same chunk style you're doing with the other word sets.

As another example, consider that you want to learn to play the guitar. What subskills would you find are more important than others? Here are a few suggestions: finger dexterity, reading music, a sense of rhythm, and hand strength. Devote a disproportionate amount of time to these individual facets, and your overall guitar skills will grow by leaps and bounds. Deconstruct, make a list, and then seek to understand which subskills are more capable of creating a domino effect.

In almost all applications, you'll find that only a relatively small number of subskills are absolutely vital to effectively practicing a larger skill. Deconstructing them and narrowing your focus can get you much further than you can imagine. You can learn the additional, less critical skills along the way once you've mastered the 20%. Not all subskills are important at all levels, and indeed, most won't be important when you are just beginning to learn a new skill. Understand what makes a difference and put your efforts where they will matter the most.

Mix Styles and Mediums

When it comes to learning, there are about a million and a half different so-called styles, methods, and mediums, each with their own cadre of advocates using supporting hypotheses. The learning pyramid might be the most infamous one that you have probably heard of (yes, that one was disproven as well). Another one might be the myth about hemispheres having different functionalities, such as the right hemisphere of the brain possessing our creative potential, while the left hemisphere houses the logical aspects. That one has also been disproven.

In reality, this is a relief because it means that information is simply information, no matter how it is presented. There is no need to engage in special formulas or techniques just to optimize learning. Whether you hear information through reading or writing makes no difference to how you process it.

This comes with a rather large caveat.

The notion of different styles and mediums still has quite a bit of merit because learning comes down to how focused you are, and how much attention you pay. That's really what determines how much information you can absorb. You can hear a lecture and read a book on the same topic, but if you are constantly distracted while reading the book, you might be better serviced with audio lessons in whatever you want to learn.

Perhaps the important lesson regarding learning styles, approaches, and mediums is that you learn the best in whatever you can pay attention to. When learning becomes tedious and boring, that's when it becomes ineffective. Therefore, we will explore a few different ways for you to absorb information. Ultimately, whatever works best for you is what you should adopt, be it from a disproven myth of learning or a scientifically proven theory. As long as it produces results, either choice is fair.

We'll talk about two models of learning that contain multiple ways of engaging with information. The first is the Solomon-Felder index of learning styles and preferences. It was created in 1996, and it consists of eight approaches to learn information. Again, the purpose is to arm you with different tools you can use, not to push one approach over others. Perhaps you can identify which of the following styles you already utilize, and consciously step outside of yourself to use the opposing one next time.

The styles, which we will discuss in greater detail are below. Just because some of the styles appear to oppose others doesn't mean that you can't feel a connection to both, or all of them.

- active versus reflective
- sensing versus intuitive

- visual versus verbal/other
- sequential versus global

Active versus reflective. An active learner obtains knowledge by doing. They're constantly interacting with what they're learning, by putting it into practice or having exchanges with others where they explain or debate about it. Reflective learners are more likely to consider the material they're learning first, analyzing and sorting it out mentally, before putting it into action. More concisely put, active learners say, "Let's do something!" while reflective learners say, "Let's think this through!"

Let's take woodworking as an example. An active learner would get all the materials they need, read through some basic instructions, and start putting a table together. They learn a lot by trial and error: finishing the wood surface, cutting pieces, and putting them all together to see how they worked. A reflective learner, on the other hand, might stop after reading the instructions and consider the geometrical strategy, analyze the different kinds of paints and stains they might use, and basically just add more levels of thoughtful planning to *understand* what they want to happen. As long as this part doesn't lead to an unacceptable amount of procrastination, that's fine.

Sensing versus intuitive. This pair of learning styles is related to the dichotomy of "detail-oriented" and "big-picture" thinkers. Sensing learners are attracted to information, memory, and traditional designs of learning—they're practical. They have an eye for specific elements in a task, itemize and follow established problem-solving procedures, and pay close attention to the particulars of a problem.

Intuitive learners, on the other hand, focus on the effects, connections, and potentials of a certain skill. They're creative and seek new prospects for understanding and relationships between concepts. They don't always pay mind to the little details and might make errors more often, but their intense understanding of the goal at hand keeps their perspective vital. They think more abstractly.

For example, a sensing learner in a web development program would focus on all the minutiae of their code. They're fastidious about reviewing each line, spotting errors, and making adjustments as needed. They'd know the intimate details of their scripts and would probably know how to fix an error quite quickly. An intuitive learner would be more focused on how certain applications and codes would work together, how the individual cogs relate to each other in service of a bigger purpose. The sensing learner sees HTML code, JavaScript, and individually executable components; the intuitive learner sees the components of an online store and tries to make them all work in sync.

Visual versus auditory versus read-writer versus kinesthetic. These styles are differentiated in the way information is presented to the learner. Visual learners, as you'd expect, respond to pictures, charts, graphics, sketches, movies, live demonstrations, and other eye-friendly media. They learn through seeing things. A visual student of social studies responds to a graph showing population distribution; a visual cooking student appreciates a tutorial video of someone making pan-fried chicken.

We classify two slightly different styles under the heading of verbal learning. Auditory learners learn through hearing and speaking, as in a lecture or discussion group. Their grasp of the Battle of Waterloo is greater when an animated professor is telling the story.

Read-write learners, on the other hand, focus on the written word, retaining information through books, research narratives, and transcripts; written reports or accounts are also their preferred output for explaining what they've learned. They'd prefer to read a book about Napoleon's defeat at Waterloo. Both auditory and read-write learners place heavy emphasis on words.

Kinesthetic learners thrive on physical activity. They need movement. Their muscles are the primary conduits for their memory; they tend to excel at hand-eye coordination, physical timing, and reaction. Obviously, kinesthetic learners tend to excel at sports, dancing, and other physical actions. But astute teachers can instruct more intellectual subjects to kinesthetic learners—for example, by encouraging them to draw diagrams or sketches of what they're learning (it keeps their hands moving).

Sequential versus global. This pair of learning approaches is parallel to sensing/intuitive. The sequential learner needs order and logical procession. They get knowledge in a linear fashion, one piece at a time, and each piece of knowledge is a reasonable extension from the one that came before. Sequential learners solve problems by following a series of ordered directions, advancing within them one by one.

Global learners are less systematic. They learn things on the fly as they occur and can't necessarily describe the smaller particulars of the subject they learn. They tend to respond to leaping learning, from topic to topic, and don't always see how each topic connects at first. But somehow they eventually "get it." Their natural inclination to learn in a more accidental way allows them to form unusual relationships between individual schools of thought and knowledge, which in turn helps them solve more intricate and complicated issues in unexpected ways.

For example, in learning how to be a better public speaker, a sequential learner would want to progress step by step. They'd take one aspect at a time: writing a speech, changing vocal tone, using gestures, reading an audience—each facet of public speaking would be revealed in logical order and dealt with one at a time. A global learner would fling themselves out there and learn in practice without pondering each step. They'd dive into public speaking and analyze their overall skills in larger groups, fine-tuning the aspects gradually, but severally.

By actively planning your learning, you are putting yourself in the best position for success. Whatever keeps your attention is what causes the best learning.

Next, we turn our sights to the learning pyramid. The learning pyramid is a well-known visual aid that ranks all learning methods in order of how much knowledge students retain using each strategy.

The pyramid suggests that students retain 5% of what they learn in a lecture, 20% from audiovisual sources, 75% in practice, and so forth. The pyramid is divided between passive and active learning, with the top four tiers of lecture, reading, audiovisual learning, and demonstration identified as "passive." The bottom three layers of discussion, practice, and teaching others are described as "active."

It's theoretical, and most education experts dispute its applicability across the board. There is no real concrete, scientific proof that the learning pyramid is accurate.

Nevertheless, I like the idea. There's nothing in the explanation of the learning pyramid that seems outrageously wrong, and I agree that mixing up mediums of learning is a very a good idea. Again, it comes down to what keeps you engaged and focused, and the more active the type of learning, the more engaged you will be. Use all of the types of learning in the pyramid and you are bound to absorb information better—even if only out of novelty and surprise!

Here's a breakdown of each of the tiers of the pyramid.

Listening to lectures (5% retention). The type of learning that has the least effect on memorization is the good ole professor standing at the lectern. This way of learning is increasingly becoming trivial as technology advances. I'm not entirely convinced that's not just an excuse for not showing up to class, but I understand the thinking.

In the specific area of skill acquisition, there aren't a lot of situations where classic lectures are an integral component— perhaps a class instructor explaining the spiritual background of yoga or an auto shop teacher explaining how an engine works. Generally, discourses about the theory of a certain skill are limited to the very beginning of your instruction. Theory is helpful and important to know, but only for background, context, and general comprehension of significance.

Reading (10% retention). There's no question that reading books about a certain subject, especially ones about the skill you're learning, is a vital component. You can find plenty of publications that contain valuable information: how-to books on carpentry, step-by-step manuals on self-defense, strategic volumes on real estate negotiating, even regular periodicals on fishing and landscaping. It's always better to have too much information handy than not enough.

But all the reading in the world by itself may not help you master a skill. You'll have to put it into practice. Even though reading is defined as "passive" learning, one needs to make it as active as one can by connecting the material you're reading to your own ideas, observations, and life experiences. That's true for all reading.

Audio/visual learning (20% retention). This is learning by watching or listening to programs about your topic of interest—perhaps books on tape about political history for those trying to build up debate skills, or YouTube demonstration videos on cooking.

You can access enough audio-visual material over your phone and laptop—even your car. It's certainly true that online course modules like Udemy and Coursera offer A/V materials in a very organized fashion for the topic or skill you want to learn. I'm skeptical it's that much more memorable than active reading, but I agree that, as a passive learning plank, it's a good one. Strictly defined, a skill is *doing something*, so it's great to watch someone because it's easier to directly emulate them.

Demonstration (30% retention). This is the live performance of a certain task right in front of you, like a cooking demonstration at a supermarket or welding wires together with a soldering iron. Demonstrations are the heart of private lesson teachers and adult classes. They're obviously more memorable than prerecorded A/V materials because they happen right in your presence and you can actually ask questions of the person doing the demonstration. It's a big building block of mentoring and coaching, where you're shown how to do something and then compelled to do it yourself.

Group discussion (50% retention). This is the first example of active learning in the pyramid, where you converse with a few others who are learning the skill you're taking up. This could be a round-table with green thumbs who are trying to build a vegetable garden from scratch, or a group of Spanish language students who get together and practice with each other. You are able to exchange ideas and thoughts, and clear up misconceptions as they occur. You can compare experiences. A writing group, for example, can reveal how other writers approach the same subject from different points of view, raising questions about the subject you may not have thought about.

In particular, discussing your skill with people of different levels—both above and u—facilitates better practicing and ...ension. When you seek to teach ... less skilled or knowledgeable, you ... ...anize your thoughts and simplify matters for yourself. When you seek to learn from someone more skilled or knowledgeable, well, that's the whole point.

Real-life experience (75% retention). Getting under the hood of the car to perform maintenance, knitting a sweater, playing piano to an audience, building a treehouse—actually using your hands to finish a task is the surest way to master it over time. These examples reinforce how your skill actually gets executed in the real world, not in a theoretical or abstract way.

You get a better understanding of the real purpose of your skill and learn first-hand how to handle stress and solve problems in an unambiguous manner. All the reading and lectures in the world won't quite do simple hands-on experience justice.

Teaching others about your real-life experience (90% retention). The learning pyramid maintains that the best way to retain what you learn is by becoming a teacher yourself, in a sense. This could be giving a talk on your experiences as a mountain climber or starting a blog about filmmaking techniques you've employed. By verbalizing your experience, you help it resound with yourself as well as others.

When you articulate the methods you use and the experience you obtain, you find out what you know and don't know in quick order. As you become aware of these issues and solve them, you're able to organize your own thoughts much more effectively than when you began.

Without a doubt, teaching is one of the most involved, participatory, and non-passive types of interactions with new information we can have. Like self-explanation and the Feynman technique (covered in a later chapter), teaching someone not only roots information in your mind; it forces you to see what you truly can explain and what you can't. Teaching yourself is good; teaching others is even better.

Teaching exposes the gaps in your knowledge. Having to instruct and explain doesn't let you hide behind generalizations: "Yeah, I know all about how that works. I'll skip it for now." That won't fly if you're explaining a process to someone else—you have to know how every step works and how each step relates to another. You'll also be forced to answer questions about the information you're teaching.

Having to explain what's going on is essentially a test of your knowledge, and you either know it or you don't. If you can't explain to someone how to replicate something you are teaching, then you actually don't know it.

Let's take photography as an example. According to the learning pyramid, reading and lecturing combined take up 15% of your retained knowledge, which makes sense: there's only so much you can learn about photography from a textbook or a lectern. Audio-visual aids and seeing demonstrations—what certain angles look like, how to use computers to filter a print—are yet more helpful in learning to take and process certain pictures. A group discussion about photography would unlock some memorable ideas, and of course, spending the time to practice taking and developing pictures makes solid impressions on your experience.

Now let's examine the bottom (or top, depending on your view) part of the pyramid related to teaching others. You're reinforcing the basic knowledge in others and explaining the principles, types, and general guidelines of photography. Theoretically, you're overseeing all the upper (or lower) segments of the pyramid for students and using your knowledge of the photography process as a guidepost for all of them. And this doesn't even include the pre-instruction time when you're preparing for your own class.

All those teaching activities are active agents that call upon what you already know—and the act of pulling something *out* of your brain rather than putting stuff *into* it turns out to be incredibly important in learning, skill acquisition, memory, and any type of improvement.

That's exactly what's happening with the higher levels of the pyramid. You're extracting from your previously learned knowledge, interpreting it, and reshaping it for others to understand and learn. In turn, that reinforces what you know and deepens your experience a little in the process.

It's common that you even surprise yourself and find additional insights by explaining and reasoning out loud in a way that simplifies and condenses. Teaching forces you to create bite-sized chunks and teach replication—a task you may find far different than explaining theories or concepts.

Using these methods and mediums in combination, both from the learning pyramid and the Solomon-Felder index of learning preferences, and getting them to play well together can make for a compelling learning experience that will enrich your understanding, skill, and talent.

Say you want to learn to make sushi. Start with cookbooks and lectures on the theory and history of sushi. Sprinkle in some

YouTube videos that show sushi preparation on camera, and check out the documentary *Jiro Dreams of Sushi*, which depicts the daily life of one of the greatest sushi chefs in Japan. Any aspiring sushi chef must also attend an up-close demonstration and class, and no doubt you'll be doing some hands-on efforts in that class as well. You can discuss techniques with other people in your class. And when you've gotten enough experience under your belt, you could attempt to teach your friends how to make sushi, or make videos yourself.

Joining together all of these various activities into an organized plan is a near-certain way to ensure effective learning and eventual expertise in a skill.

Gather Information and Resources

An integral part of planning for learning is gathering the resources you'll be staring at or listening to for hours. This is actually a slightly harder process than you think it is for a simple reason: you don't know who you can trust these days.

An expert may hold themselves out to be so, but what makes them an expert besides the title on their business card? Or, you might see a bona fide expert, but what makes them good at teaching a skill or conveying information? Or, despite this person being intelligent and articulate, what if they are in the extreme minority view of a position or stance?

So, one can spend an unlimited amount of time, resources, and money getting every bit of information that's relevant to the skill you've decided upon. There are instruction manuals, online tutorials, courses, discussions with experts and coaches, diagrams, blueprints, illustrations—the complete gamut. So should you consume all of it?

No! So you need to do some preliminary research that narrows down your resources to the best ones. You should focus on credibility, acceptance, and clarity when finding your resources. After you read around a bit, you'll find that some things are repeated often while others spout nonsense that others won't mention. You should be able to slowly triangulate on the credible sources thusly.

Research is a gradual process. It's methodical and investigative. The next five steps of research, if executed thoughtfully and correctly, will give you what you need to gain firm command over a new topic. It's important to hit all five steps without skipping any. You'll be able to understand a concept, issue, or problem from a variety of angles and approaches.

1. Gather information. The first step is to retrieve as much data about a topic as you possibly can. Collect anything and everything from as wide a range of sources as you can manage.

At this early stage of research, don't be too discriminating. Get as much as you can from wherever you can find it. Think what it would be like if you searched on Google about a certain topic, got 10 pages or more of results, and clicked on every single link. The point isn't to get immediate answers; it's to get an initial, panoramic overview of the subject you're investigating. So don't be too restrictive—open the floodgates. Organize the information you gather into general topics, arguments, and opinions. You might find that you are more confused after this stage than when you started—that's fine and natural. What's important is that you have everything in front of you, from shallow to deep and from correct to dubious.

2. Filter your sources. Now that you've got all the information you need, it's time to identify what your sources are, what kind of information they present, and whether it's good or not. This step could reduce the amount of information you'll study by 75% or even more.

Every information outlet has a different intent and approach over the subject matter it discusses. Some concentrate on hard and straight data. Some offer narrative accounts or anecdotes relating to the subject, while others offer editorial opinions or theories. Some sources are official agencies or authorities in your chosen field, while others are trade papers, media, groups, or associations who are interested in it. Some are simply blogs of opinionated people who have taken an interest in a particular topic with no expertise or common sense. And yes, some are "fake news."

Your goal here is to draw out the good sources and disregard the bad ones. A good source backs up its arguments and ideas with solid data, confirmable truth, and careful examination. A bad source is generally more interested in persuading through emotions and hyperbole and might rely on misleading or utterly wrong data to do so.

Don't confuse anecdote with evidence, even if there are multiple anecdotes. After all, that's how every single old wives' tale was started.

At this stage, you'll start noticing some divisions in the research you've collected. You'll see certain sources' tendencies and inclinations. You'll get a sense of which are the most popular or common outlooks (the majority), which are the rarer or more unusual viewpoints (the minority), and which ones are straight-up crazy ramblings from the minds of lunatics (the crackpots). You'll be able to divide up the sources and retain the ones that are most reliable and helpful.

3. Look for patterns and overlap. As you're viewing and reviewing all your source material, you'll begin to notice recurring topics, stances, and ideas. Certain points will crop up more frequently, and some will only appear once, seemingly randomly. You'll start getting a better idea of the primary points, secondary points, and boundaries of the subject you're looking into. You'll also be able to build bridges between parallel ideas and points of overlap.

Here you'll be able to identify the major components of your topic and the most prevalent thoughts and beliefs. Generally, the best sources will talk about the same things, so when that happens, you can safely assume they're the most important parts of your subject. When you see a point repeated by multiple sources, it's a good sign that you should consider it a major point or theme. Likewise, if you see things rarely mentioned by notable people in the field or that don't fit into the prevalent views, you know it's probably not something that moves the needle or is too new to be considered valuable.

This isn't to say less common or alternative points of view are necessarily wrong—they aren't. But use your better judgment. If only one isolated source is making a certain assertion, even if they have "disciples" who agree with all they say, there's a much higher chance that they're discussing something that's not really true or at least not very important.

You should understand what the main points and arguments are (and why), as well as a few of the minor ones, by the end of this step. Getting through this stage alone may qualify you as an expert relative to others, and it's common that most people stop their journey and education here. But if you stop here, you risk falling prey to *confirmation bias* and not knowing what you don't know.

4. Seek dissenting opinions. By this point, you'll no doubt have a theory or opinion in mind. You'll also have whittled down your sources to support that. So now's the time to look for sources that disagree with you. This is a hugely important step. Without knowing the full extent of opposing arguments, you won't have the complete picture that you need to understand the issue. No matter how convinced you are, try to find one.

Don't be afraid to question your own viewpoints by playing devil's advocate. If there's a minor quibble you have about your theory, this is the point where you indulge your imagination. Imagine all possible scenarios and circumstances where your theory might be put to the test.

Finding dissenting opinions is an important step in avoiding the all-too-common plague of confirmation bias—our human tendency to hear and see only what we want to hear and see. This is when someone dearly wants for a certain thing to be true, so they reject any solid evidence that it's false and only accept information that confirms their beliefs. That leads them to cherry-pick data that supports their point and ignore hard proof that disproves it. Confirmation bias is not objective, so it has no place in actual research. To combat it, give the voice of the opposition clear and full attention.

At this point, you may arrive at a conclusion that's been put through the paces. You have sophistication and nuance. The point is legitimate and not clouded by fallacies, misunderstanding, or disinformation. You'll comprehend your own beliefs more fully and understand why others may have different ideas. You'll be able to articulate precisely why you believe what you believe.

5. Put it all together. This is the point where you make your statement—only after you've considered all the above, rather than "shooting first and asking questions later." This is a point of clarity for you. You can explain all aspects of the topic or issue you're talking about. Write, speak, outline, or mind-map confidently about your new area of knowledge. Here's an easy way to think about how you summarize your expertise: put everything together to show

how you understand the whole situation, including the small and nuanced points: "X, Y, and Z because... *however,* A, B, and C because..." If you can't do this with certainty, you may need to go back a step or two in the process.

When you're able to sniff out legitimate versus unreliable sources, you've conquered the biggest problem in regard to the research stage.

However, you might run right into the next one: the feeling that you never have enough information. This is where gathering information like a dragon gathers gold coins becomes your comfort zone—it is easier, after all, than the next step, which is to meticulously learn and study.

This is when you use planning as procrastination. It's tricky because you *think* you're working, but in truth it's just another way of delaying getting your hands dirty. It's easy to become an information junkie. In fact, it's almost harder *not* to become one.

Know that you'll never know everything. In learning a new skill, there's always a point where you have to stop or pause your intake of knowledge and take some sort of action. They are entirely separate things and often you will have to make the choice to choose action over learning.

For you, that means that at some point you'll feel like you must leap before you look. Success means knowing when to take action, even when your knowledge about the skill is less than complete. You don't have to know the ins and outs of every position on a football team to start working out. You don't need a complete knowledge of the works of Shakespeare to start writing.

Don't be afraid to jump into the fire without complete knowledge or information. You'll learn more by launching and taking action than you will from just being an armchair analyst. So many questions can only be answered with personal, firsthand experience.

Most of us are conditioned to be consumers of information. That's why it's a good idea to adopt the opposite frame of mind: the *producer* mindset. This is the realization that the initiative to move forward is something that starts within *you*, not something that comes from the outside that you're just waiting to show up. Producers get to work because they know they have something inside them, no matter how raw or undefined, that they can move forward with—and they don't wait for an external confirmation to do so. This mindset promotes activity and disables the excuses of passivity. What you don't know you'll learn along the way.

Takeaways:

- For optimal learning, plan to deconstruct your skill into smaller subskills. This helps you psychologically as it is easier to face a series of small tasks versus one large task. It also helps you use your time wisely because when you deconstruct, you can figure out which subskills or areas of inquiry have the biggest impact. This is exemplified by the 80/20 Rule—just like in learning languages, where the majority of daily conversations only use a few hundred vocabulary words.

- Be willing to learn and mix styles and mediums of learning. Though the jury is certainly out on the scientific efficacy of stylistic differences, the reality is that learning can only occur when you can pay sufficient attention and maintain adequate focus. That's just harder in some mediums and styles for some people over others. There's no downside to having different types of ammunition for learning. There are two models we talk about: the learning pyramid (reading, listening, doing, teaching, etc.), and the Solomon-Felder index of learning styles (active, passive, global, sequential, etc.).

- The final (or for some, primary) aspect to creating a plan for learning is to understand how to effectively gather information and filter resources. After all, not all sources are created equal. This consists of a few steps involving looking for dissenting information, looking at overall trends and patterns, and constructing a nuanced overview. During this phase, many people get stuck on the information-gathering phase, and it inhibits them from action. Know that you will never know everything, and you must consciously choose to stop learning at some point.

Chapter 3. It's Just Practice

You're at the point where you're ready to start working more proactively on your skill. You've drafted your plan, you've collected your resources, and you know what you need to do. The only thing left to do is to, well, *do*.

It sounds like the easiest and simplest part of the plan toward skill acquisition—just practice and take action. It can be, but it requires you to be diligent in how you go about it. As long as you stay within some of the guidelines put forth in this next chapter, you can feel free to just *do*.

We'll examine how to institute a consistent routine, how to gain self-awareness and understand your blind spots and shortcomings, and how to make information stick in your brain and muscles the most effectively.

As a preliminary matter, in all things having to do with practice, rehearsal, and learning, it turns out that they are all more effective when done as a type of self-test, rather than mindless reviewing and highlighting. This is the difference between active recall (self-tests) and passive review (reviewing and regurgitating). This is one of the primary reasons why flash cards are so effective.

In a seminal study on active recall from 2008 by Jeffrey Karpicke of Purdue University, a group of students were given vocabulary words to learn. Students who used active recall remembered 80% of the new words versus 34% for the group who only passively reviewed the words. It seems there is something to be said for struggling and grappling with something, and then finally succeeding with it. Keep this in mind as you practice and rehearse—it's not supposed to be easy. If it is, it's not doing what you want it to.

In fact, our first point is on the very point of repeating what's hardest and drilling it.

Deliberate Practice

This is the first step toward truly excelling at your desired skill.

Deliberate practice is purposeful and systematic. Regular practice or rehearsal might entail review, repetition, and rote motions, but deliberate practice requires focused attention with the specific goal of improving performance as a whole. This is because the natural tendency of the human brain is to transform repeated behaviors into unconscious habits, and thus we must ensure that each of our behaviors is exactly what we want.

For example, when you first learned to tie your shoes, you had to think very carefully about each step of the process. If you learned it incorrectly at first, it was probably difficult to change to a more correct method. Then, over time, you don't even have to think about it—as it becomes more natural, we can process the sequence of operations automatically. But you had to correct that error, otherwise the knot would never stay tied.

To use deliberate practice, you first break your skill down into smaller components. This is something we're already familiar with from the previous chapter on deconstructing. The next part is different from any other practice you've ever conducted: you go through the motions a few times to see where you keep faltering. Those parts (whether a phase of a skill, or a topic you keep forgetting) are what you should focus on and drill repeatedly.

Putting deliberate practice to work in learning is not hard—just tedious and detail-oriented. Computer science professor Cal Newport described how he mastered discrete mathematics. This branch of math study, *very* briefly stated, involves finding proofs for theories. Newport explained how he bought reams of white paper and then copied each "proposition" the professor would present at the top of each class session.

On his own, away from the classroom, Newport worked on the proofs. When he came to a concept he didn't understand, he consulted textbooks and online sources, in his own words, "to see if I could make sense of what I was writing down." Usually the process secured Newport's understanding of the problem; if it didn't, Newport consulted with his professor for feedback.

Near the end of the course, Newport had accumulated a massive stack of handwritten proofs. He "aggressively reviewed" them. He classified his proofs into ones that he could recall with little effort and those he needed to drill down. He continued to study the problematic ones—repetitively, exhaustively—until he finally extracted the last bit of understanding from them. After his final exam, Newport was told he'd achieved the highest grade in the entire class—not just on the final but in the whole course.

This is deliberate practice in action: surveying the landscape, identifying the problem areas, repetitively and aggressively examining it, and continued tests of your competency or understanding. Newport found what he was lacking, drilled without mercy, and then made sure his understanding was complete. When you identify your overall goal as improved performance, it becomes clear on how to practice to build expertise. You are only as strong as your weakest links, so you must first address them.

Let's take the familiar example of playing a new piano piece. There are a few sections in the middle where your hands don't seem to be working in sync. Normal practice might dictate that you keep zipping through the entire song, despite the fact that you have some trouble spots in the middle and everything else is already proficient. That's what most of us will do! But this is not the best use of your time. Deliberate practice demands that you drop everything else and drill the weakness in the middle until it reaches a certain level. It takes a skill component by component and ensures that each phase is up to par—only then will overall performance be adequate.

Most any skill be mastered using this intensive technique—there's really no prohibition on what you can learn through deliberate practice.

The enemy of deliberate practice is mindless activity and motion for motion's sake, and the danger of practicing the same thing over and over is that we'll *assume* we're making progress merely because we're gaining experience and additional exposure. But in truth, all we're doing is reinforcing our current *bad* habits—we're not improving or changing them. Don't confuse improvement with repetition because they are far from being the same. Improvement comes with repetition, but repetition by itself is worthless in your pursuit of rapid skill acquisition. Additional points in effective practice include the following:

Practice sessions. There is an optimal amount of time you should practice, believe it or not. Many studies say that our energy levels correspond to daily cycles, and they mirror the 90-minute duration of REM sleep cycles. But the truth is, the perfect length of a practice or study session will differ for everyone. Make sure you aren't practicing so long that you are burning out, but you are practicing long enough that you aren't bored or disengaged and don't allow yourself to "get into the zone". Anything else just becomes repetition. In fact, you should ensure that you stop before your practice begins to get sloppy because of the next point.

Muscle memory sees what it sees. In other words, it doesn't discriminate between what is good practice and what is bad practice. Consequently, it doesn't discriminate between good and bad habits—they just remember what they are exposed to. This is why mistakes can be so difficult to crack; they are as much a part of your memory as the good parts. Perfect practice makes perfect skills, so this compounds on each of the earlier points on learning slowly, practicing well, and stopping before you get sloppy.

On the same note, slow down your learning. Start slow, learn slow, and don't let your impatience get the best of you. When you learn slow, you put yourself in the best position for success because everything is done correctly and accurately. If you don't learn slow, you'll find that you often can't slow down later—because you have not adequately learned the intermediate steps involved. Increase your tempo later—what's the rush?

Patience. As if you needed to be reminded of patience again. But acquiring a skill is more than simply swinging a racket or understanding why your fingers should move a certain way. It is the process of building muscle memory, and research has indicated that it can take up to 1000 repetitions on the lower end for simpler skills and 30,000 repetitions on the higher end for more complex skills to be cemented and become second nature. Let's suppose you play a difficult piano piece for an hour a day. You can get through the piece 20 times in that hour. Even if you shoot for 1000 repetitions, that's not going to be a short amount of time any way you slice it. So be as patient as possible and manage your expectations.

Interleaved Practice

This method of practice is much different from what you might have previously considered gospel: devoting time to learning one subject in uninterrupted blocks, like eating all of your vegetables first before eating your dessert. It turns out this isn't the optimal way for the brain or muscles to absorb information.

Using uninterrupted blocks involves learning or practicing one skill at a time before progressing to another one. You don't move on from working on one skill until you've completed the routine—you finish Skill A before Skill B and finish Skill B before moving on to Skill C. Representing study time units as one letter, this practice would establish a pattern that looks like AAABBBCCC.

Interleaving disrupts that sequence. It mixes the practice of several related skills throughout a single study session. Where a typical study session might look like AAA, an interleaved study session would look more like ABC.

For example, a beginning algebra student may be tasked with comprehending exponents, graphing, and radicals. Instead of taking each subject one at a time, they could start with exponents, break off and practice graphing, then work on the radicals of square roots, and then go back to studying exponents. When studying Shakespeare, one could divide portions of a study session by switching between the playwright's comedies, tragedies, and historical plays. Taking it to another level, you could study Shakespeare, then mathematics, and then African history all in the same study block.

Interleaved practice at first might seem a haphazard, somewhat randomized way of learning in comparison. It might also seem that you just can't synthesize information when you interrupt its percolating in your brain so frequently. But which method actually works best? Research indicates that interleaving is actually much more effective for motor learning and cognitive tasks.

Its advantage over block learning is surprising: interleaving produces a 43% increase in learning and retention over block learning. There are a few reasons for this.

First, interleaving pushes a student out of their comfort zone. Remember that the harder the practice, the more effective the learning generally is. Second, interleaving breaks any patterns and familiarity you have with a certain topic in isolation. This disruption forces you to practice active recall more, and leaves you unable to passively review information.

Third, and perhaps most importantly, the blending of concepts or problems builds and reinforces stronger connections between them. Students generally perceive concepts and skills as free-standing, self-contained bits of information with no apparent or obvious connections to other bits. But the more often we can connect information or skills with other things we already know, the more likely we are to understand and remember the information (Blaisman, 2017). Regularly interleaving material and skills facilitates discovery of these connections and encourages us to find unexpected bridges for ultimately better retention between different skills and ideas.

The benefits of interleaved practice are two-fold. First, it improves the brain's ability to discriminate between concepts. In blocking, once you know what the solution is, the hard part's over. With interleaving, each practice varies from the last, so rote or automated responses don't work. Instead, your brain has to continually focus on finding different solutions. This process sharpens your ability to learn critical features of skills and concepts, which therefore helps you select the correct response and execute it.

Interleaving also strengthens memory associations. In blocking, you only need to hold one strategy in your short-term memory at a time. In interleaving, the strategy will always be different because the solution changes from one attempt to the next. Your brain is relentlessly engaged in calling forth different responses and bringing them into your short-term memory. Again, it's an active and more challenging approach—but it reinforces your neural connections among different tasks and responses, which enhances and improves learning.

The most important tip to remember is that interleaving isn't the same as multitasking, which you should avoid. Don't play *too* loosely with the disciplines you're learning—interleaving between chemistry, English literature, and ceramics is probably more trouble than it's worth, not to mention messy.

Rather, within a single study session, move between multiple topics. Try to set a limit on how many different angles or subjects you'll handle in a given study block—three is enough and four might be good for intense sessions—but once you're in, feel free to let your instincts guide you from topic to topic. Setting a timer for each topic is fine, but for some, the enforcement of an artificial limit might not be ideal for comprehension purposes.

Even if the subjects you interleaf don't vary too wildly, you still have some wiggle room. For example, you can juggle readings in English literature, European architecture, and Greek philosophy without too much shock to the system. Subjects that spur the finding of connections are especially helpful—blending studies in art theory, art technique, and the history of pop cultural art of the '60s could very well produce meaning that can easily be shared across all three concepts. Similarly, working on a set of scales on your guitar, then chord progressions, then picking exercises all fall under the same umbrella and can create a sort of synergy.

As with everything we've discussed thus far, the truly most important factor in learning is how much attention you can pay, and how well you can focus. Interleaving might help keep things fresh for you, or it might prove too spastic and unable to allow you to focus in shorter periods of time. Use with caution! It doesn't necessarily matter what is scientifically proven sometimes.

Spaced Repetition

Spaced repetition—otherwise known as distributed practice—is just what it sounds like.

In order to commit more to memory and retain information better, you space out your rehearsal and exposure to it over as long of a period as possible. In other words, you learn information and skills far better if you study it for one hour each day versus 20 hours in one weekend. Similarly, research has shown that seeing something 20 times in one day is far less effective than seeing something 10 times over the course of seven days. *So much for cramming.*

What does this say about how to practice? Spaced repetition is the concept that 5 minutes a day is far superior to learning and memory than an hour a week. When you focus on *frequency* of learning versus duration or even intensity, you will learn better. Focusing on duration usually becomes motion for motion's sake, and can oftentimes become detrimental overall to your goals.

It makes more sense if you imagine your brain as a muscle. Muscles can't be exercised all the time and then put back to work with little to no recovery. Your brain needs time to make connections between concepts, create muscle memory, and generally become familiar with something. Sleep has been shown to be where neural connections are made, and it's not just mental. Synaptic connections are made in your brain and dendrites are stimulated.

If an athlete works out too hard in one session like you might be tempted to in studying, one of two things will happen. The athlete will either be too exhausted, and the latter half of the workout will have been useless, or the athlete will become injured. Rest and recovery are necessary to the task of learning, and sometimes effort isn't what's required.

So when you focus on frequency, suddenly you have a clear structure to organize your practice with. Without a plan in place, most people will just study and practice until their eyes or fingers bleed and they collapse from exhaustion, but that's not working smart, just hard. If you just follow what spaced repetition prescribes, you'll have your schedule for optimal learning set up for you.

Let's take studying for a topic you have trouble with: Spanish history. If you have trouble with this topic, that just means even more frequency should be devoted to it. A study or practice schedule focused solely on duration would be relentless from Monday to Sunday. Here's a look at what an optimized schedule focused on frequency might look like.

Monday at 10:00 a.m. Learn initial facts about Spanish history. You accumulate five pages of notes.

Monday at 8:00 p.m. Review notes about Spanish history, but don't just review passively. Make sure to try to recall the information from your own memory. Recalling is a much better way to process information than simply rereading and reviewing. This might only take 20 minutes.

Tuesday at 10:00 a.m. Try to recall the information without looking at your notes much. After you first try to actively recall as much as possible, go back through your notes to see what you missed, and make note of what you need to pay closer attention to. This will probably take only 15 minutes.

Tuesday at 8:00 p.m. Review notes. This will take 10 minutes.

Wednesday at 4:00 p.m. Try to independently recall the information again, and only look at your notes once you are done to see what else you have missed. This will take only 10 minutes. Make sure not to skip any steps.

Thursday at 6:00 p.m. Review notes. This will take 10 minutes.

Friday at 10:00 a.m. Active recall session. This will take 10 minutes.

Looking at this schedule, note that you are only studying an additional 75 minutes throughout the week but that you've managed to go through the entire lesson a whopping six additional times. Not only that, you've likely committed most of it to memory because you are using active recall instead of passively reviewing your notes. Even if you take your time to be thorough and double the overall time to 150 minutes, it's still a fraction of what you would have previously spent to do far less.

It's astonishing what you can accomplish in short periods of time if you focus on frequency and you don't allow yourself to drift. Scheduling relatively shorter time periods for material keeps you on your toes and not slipping into laziness if you were to schedule huge blocks of time for one task.

You're ready for a test the next Monday. Actually, you're ready for a test by Friday afternoon. Spaced repetition gives your brain time to process concepts and make its own connections and leaps because of the repetition.

Think about what happens when you have repeated exposure to a concept or skill. For the first couple of exposures, you may not see anything new. As you get more familiar with it and stop going through the motions, you begin to examine it on a deeper level and think about the context surrounding it. You begin to relate it to other concepts or information, and you generally make sense of it below surface level.

There is no mindless motion: it must be active and engaged—which you can only do in short spurts. Flashcards are particularly useful for this, especially if you keep shuffling them and putting them into different orders.

It also helps to pick a different starting spot in the material for each session so you are mixing up the order and aren't just going over the same spots each time. The idea is to keep injecting freshness and different perspectives on the same material that you're seeing multiple times a day.

All of this is designed to push information from your short-term memory into your long-term memory. That's why cramming or studying at the last minute isn't an effective means of learning. Very little tends to make it into long-term memory because of the lack of repetition and deeper analysis. At that point, it becomes rote memorization instead of the concept learning we discussed earlier, which is destined to fade far more quickly.

Hopefully from this point on, instead of measuring the number of hours you spend on something, try instead to measure the number of times you can revisit it. Make it your goal to increase the frequency of reviewing, not necessarily the duration. Ideally you have both, but the literature on spaced repetition makes clear that breathing room is more important.

Spaced repetition generally has two different uses. You can use it for initial learning, but you can also use it to prevent forgetting and to ensure things stick in your brain. The above example was focused on the initial learning phase, but a sample schedule to prevent forgetting and simply keep things in mind will look a bit lighter. It will strategically touch upon information just enough to keep it in your mind, but not too much as to waste time or hit the point of diminishing returns (which is when you have already memorized it).

For example: Monday: 12pm, Wednesday: 12pm, Saturday: 12pm. Our brains don't necessarily want to remember more than is necessary and will dump information at the first opportunity, so spaced refreshing is far superior than one large block of time on one day.

Imagine a path in a garden that gets worn with time. The path is a memory in your brain, and it takes a certain amount of repetitions to become deep enough to stand on its own. Even a few repetitions can make a huge difference as to how clear the path becomes and how long the path will last.

If you're really pressed for time, just know that studying something twice is better than once, almost always. If you want to improve your memory and skill instantly, review something for 15 minutes before you sleep, at the end of your day. That's all it takes to get a head start on others and learn better. Just in case you are looking for a more step by step guideline on using spaced repetition and optimizing for frequency, here are four points.

> 1. Copy my study plan regarding Spanish history. Seven times a week sounds like a lot, but in reality, it ends up only being an extra 1-2 hours. This helps you keep focus, and capitalizes on the way your brain prefers to absorb information. Calibrate your plan to whether you are in the initial learning phase, or the "don't forget" phase.
> 2. Prioritize frequency. At least once a day, but ideally twice a day over the course of a week. Measure in terms of

how many times you can get through the material, repetitions, and not how long you spend on it. Again, calibrate this to whether you are in the learning phase, or the "don't forget" phase.

3. Engage with the material each time and don't just go through the motions. This might require you to create different and creative ways to look at the same thing over and over. As mentioned, you can use different starting points, different flashcards, and overall different ways of reading the same material over and over. Vary the input method here.

4. Test yourself. Don't skip over things, and don't just review, read, or recognize. If it feels too easy, you aren't learning optimally.

The first three sections of this chapter likely present the idea of mere practice in a far different light than you are used to. But hopefully instead of creating the feeling of dread, it creates the feeling of unleashed potential as you realize what you *haven't* been taking advantage of.

Problem-Based Learning

This next method is something we can inject into our study and practice sessions that will ensure that you are staying engaged and sufficiently challenged. It's another way of injecting freshness and investment in what you want to learn.

There is an urban legend about novice metalworkers. Their teachers tell them to carve a complex structure out of a solid block of metal with only hand tools at their disposal. After they complete this tedious and seemingly impossible problem, what do you suppose was accomplished by the student? They became true experts with hand tools.

What about famous Mr. Miyagi from *The Karate Kid* movie? Who can forget how he taught his student, Daniel-san, how to perform hard labor? And yet, after this goal was achieved, it turns out Daniel-san learned the basics of karate.

Through solving a problem or reaching for a goal, learning was made inevitable.

Problem-based learning (PBL) is where you start with a problem that needs to be solved, and you force learning through the process of solving that problem. You try to accomplish a goal that necessitates learning. Instead of setting out to learn X, the idea is to set a goal of solving problem Y, and in the process, learn X.

Usually, we learn information and skills in a linear manner. In school, a traditional approach is commonly used: material is given to us, we memorize it, and we are shown how that information solves a problem. This might even be how you structure your learning when you're by yourself—because you don't know different.

PBL requires you to identify what you already know about the problem and what knowledge and resources you still need, to figure out how and where to obtain that new information, and finally how to piece together a solution to the problem. This is far different from the linear approach of most schooling. We can draw on my failed romantic escapades as an adolescent for illustration.

I wanted to impress *Jessica from Spanish class*. It's a noble and mighty motivation that has been the impetus for many changes in the life of a young (and old) male. We were in the same Spanish class and I had the good fortune of sitting directly behind her. It turns out she wasn't too interested in Spanish, so she would constantly turn around and ask me for help.

I would first get caught in her eyes, but then my spirits would fall because I realized I had no idea how to answer her questions. *What if she started asking the other guys in the class? I didn't want that!*

With that in mind, I began to study and learn Spanish so she would have all the more reason to continue turning around and talking to me. It's amazing what you can do when you have the proper motivation for it, and I probably became fluent more quickly than anyone in the class that year. What's more, I would look up obscure or complex phrases and words solely to impress her, just in case I had the opportunity.

I created a massive set of flashcards. They started with one word on the back of each card, but by the end of the school year, they had three to four sentences on back of each, all in Spanish. I got an A+ in the class, one of the few in my high school career, but I never did get anywhere with Jessica.

This is a classic case of PBL—I wanted to solve the problem of X (Jessica), but I ended up learning Y (Spanish) in the process.

Of course, the key for us is to be deliberate about the problem you spend your time solving, so what you learn helps you accomplish what you want. It can be as simple as wanting to learn a new scale on the guitar, and attempting to play a difficult song that incorporates that scale. You can see how focusing on solving a problem can be more helpful and educational than simply reading a textbook or hearing a lecture. There's certainly something to be said for firsthand experience.

PBL has been around in one form or another since John Dewey's pivotal 1916 book *Democracy and Education: An Introduction to the Philosophy of Education*. One of the basic premises of Dewey's book was learning by doing.

Fast forward to the 1960s when PBL had its modern start. Medical schools started using real patient cases and examples to train future doctors. Indeed, this is still how many medical students learn to diagnose and treat patients. Rather than memorize an endless supply of facts and figures, medical students went through the diagnostic process and picked up the knowledge and information along the way. That's a different muscle than reading and writing notes.

What questions should they ask of the patient? What information do they need from the patient? What tests should be run? What do the results of those tests mean? How do the results determine the course of treatment?

Imagine that a medical student is presented with the following case: A 66-year-old male patient comes in to the office complaining of recent shortness of breath. What are the next steps in this blank canvas?

In addition to medical, family, and social histories, they would want to find out how long the symptoms have been occurring, what time of day, what activities lead to shortness of breath, does anything make it worse or better? The physical exam, then, becomes problem-focused: check blood pressure, listen to heart and lungs, check legs for edema, etc. Next the student would determine whether any lab tests or x-rays need to be done. And then based on those results, the student would come up with a plan for treatment. And that's just for starters.

If the instructor wanted the student to learn about how to deal with potential heart problems, they accomplished that. By applying their investigative skills to real-world cases, the learning was more realistic, more memorable, and more engaging for the medical students. Research has shown that when learning is problem-based for medical students, clinical reasoning and problem solving skills improve, learning is more in-depth, and concepts are integrated for better overall understanding of the material.

It forces people to take ownership of the solution and approach, and they absorb a concept or set of information in an entirely different manner. Instead of knowing that they are simply solving for X, they must come up with the entire equation that leads to X. It involves a deep sense of exploration and analysis, both of which lead to a greater understanding than simple regurgitation.

Greater self-motivation is seen as well because rather than learning for learning's sake, there is a real-life issue at stake, with real-life consequences.

Living in the "real world," we typically aren't given case scenarios or assigned to group projects (at least not in the elementary school sense of the phrase) to assist in our learning goals. Whether we know it or not, we can put ourselves in a position to enhance our learning by directing it to specific purposes. What follows are a few examples of how to find a problem that will necessitate further learning on your part.

Meal Planning. For instance, you want to solve a problem about dealing with delayed and frantic dinners. You choose this because, besides solving the problem of unnecessary stress and anxiety, you will be able to learn how to become a better cook in every sense of the word. You want to solve X (stressful meals) but along the way also learn Y (how to cook better).

So, what steps would you take to become more proficient in the kitchen? One way would be to implement a meal planning system to allow you to try new recipes and techniques. Well, what do you already know about the problem? Your family needs to eat. Recipes would be nice, perhaps starting out easy and then becoming more involved. You need the ingredients to make those recipes, a schedule of what meal to serve when, and a strategy for how you will learn the more advanced techniques.

What do you still need to know? You need actual recipes and ingredient lists. You need some sort of organized plan for when you'll serve each dinner, probably a calendar. You may want to identify specific skills you want to acquire.

Where will you obtain new information to help solve this problem? Maybe you start by asking members of your family to share their three favorite meals with you. Then you hop on Pinterest to find some recipes. From there, you make a grocery list, maybe on a notepad, or your computer in a Word doc, or a grocery app you find. Next you need to put your meals onto a calendar.

Again, you may do this on your computer or you might find a meal planning printable or app. And maybe you want to explore online grocery ordering with delivery or pick-up to further save time (and probably impulse spending). You'll need to figure out how you will learn new cooking approaches: reading, YouTube videos, going to a class, etc.

By making a strategic plan to enhance your cooking skills, you have solved your mealtime chaos by using PBL! You identified what you already knew (you need ideas about what new skills you wanted to learn, meal ideas, recipes, a grocery list), figured out what you still needed to know (the techniques themselves, specific recipes, ingredient lists, a meal calendar), and where you found that information (family, Pinterest, apps, books, online, computer, etc.).

Not only have you created a plan for your family's upcoming meals, you have devised a strategy to use moving forward week after week, month after month, all the while being able to learn new techniques and improving your cooking skills. By developing a meal planning strategy, you are saving time and money, and you may see a decrease in chaos and an increase in family satisfaction with meals. Call it killing two birds with one stone.

The Broken Toaster. Let's consider a more complicated problem. Your toaster seems to no longer be working, and you have toast for breakfast every day. You've always wanted to learn more about electronics and put to use what you learned years ago. You want to solve X (broken toaster) but along the way also learn Y (basic electronics skills). What would PBL look like in this somewhat daunting scenario?

The first step is to determine what you already know. Your toaster isn't functioning. You're pretty handy and would consider fixing it yourself. You know a little about wiring. And you really like your toaster, a model that is no longer made.

What, then, do you need to know to solve this problem? You will need to determine the specific cause of your toaster malfunction. You will potentially need some instruction for aspects of the problem outside your current skill set. You will need tools and supplies as well as the time and a place to work on your toaster.

In the information-gathering stage, you will disassemble your toaster to try to determine the problem. You may look online or go to the library for a "fix-it" manual for small appliances. There are YouTube videos you could consult for a visual tutorial. Then, once you've determined the issue, learned how to fix it, and made the repair, you're back in business with your toaster.

Problem-Based Learning provides a helpful framework for a thoughtful, organized way to approach a problem, challenge, or dilemma in order to learn a new skill or new information. You can think of PBL as a series of steps as demonstrated in the examples above.

1. Define your problem.

2. Determine what you already know.
3. List potential solutions and choose the one most likely to succeed.
4. Break the steps into action items (a timeline often helps).
5. Identify what you still need to know and how you will get that information.

There are some distinct advantages to PBL. Not only will you have better retention of what you have learned, you will generally have a deeper understanding of the problem and solutions than if you had taken a less focused approach. While it can seem like a problem-based approach has too many steps and will take too long, generally PBL tends to save you time in the long run since you aren't randomly trying less well thought out solution after solution. The planning and systematic plan ultimately saves you time, and often money, too! That is the benefit of directly solving a problem—you get to the heart of what matters.

PBL can be applied to most any aspect of your life. You may have to get creative in how to design a problem or goal around something you want to learn, but this is the type of learning technique that will skyrocket your progress. After all, there's only so much we can gain without applying what you know to the real world.

"When you lose, don't lose the lesson."

Practice is hard work—at least, *proper* practice is.

But there's an important and severely underrated part of practice that most people ignore, and that's simply determining how the practice, review, or rehearsal actually went. Are you actually improving on your guitar solos, memorizing the countries of the world better, or singing better than before? What is the difference from before?

Without a coach, teacher, or mentor figure, most of us aren't able to solicit the immediate type of feedback that is necessary. This requires us to perform one of the most difficult tasks of all—to pay attention to ourselves. Learning is never entirely linear and successful—you go in one direction, you get shoved into a slightly more correct course, and this repeats itself for years sometimes until you can do this yourself.

It's even harder in the context of learning and practicing because intentions and thoughts are unimportant to achieving our goal. Actions speak louder than words and are ultimately what matter, and we have a hard time separating the two. Worse yet, is it possible to have total self-awareness when we inevitably have blind spots on ourselves?

Consider a near-disaster from when I was learning to drive many years ago. My instructor and I were driving down a busy street in the suburbs. Going at the blistering speed of 25 miles per hour, the instructor told me to signal and merge into the lane on my left. We'd worked on it a little bit, but this was the first time we were trying it on a public street, which upped the ante. *This* was the big show.

I signaled, looked back over my shoulder to see that the left lane was clear, and began to gingerly move the car into the lane. That's when I heard a loud honk. There *was* a car in the lane that I was about to run into—it was just out of my line of sight, a little behind my car in a blind spot.

Already jumpy and anxious, I overreacted to the honk and swerved violently to the right, where I nearly cut off *another* car that was going a little fast for my tastes. I got a honk from that car as well. Best of all, we were just a few feet away from an intersection where the light had *just* turned red.

With all this action happening, it hadn't yet occurred to me that the car came equipped with brakes. Instead, just as the light turned red, I stepped on the gas. A car that was eager to start a left-hand turn nearly crashed into us. At this juncture, the driving instructor thought it was a good idea to use the special brake he had installed on the passenger side so that he could take temporary control of the car.

This all happened in a sequence of about 10 seconds. Nobody got hit and there was no damage. But that's the impact a blind spot in our own self-assessment can also have—you think you might be ignoring something small in your learning or performance, only for it to have dreadful consequences down the line.

Even if you are working with a mentor or coach who will spot these flaws and take care of them, you should get into the practice of self-appraisal. For one thing, your coach won't always be available. And the more you can successfully inspect and evaluate on your own, the more of an expert you'll become. To that end, there are 10 questions that provide a progressive and effective sketch of how to assess yourself in the practice of learning a new skill. We can use the example of my near-death experience to illustrate. Not all of them will apply to each situation, and some may overlap.

1. What was the cause of the mistake? The original event in the sequence that caused all this confusion was when I tried to merge into the left-hand lane, where I didn't see a car that was in my blind spot.

2. Did you make a mistake in the strategy or the method that you chose to follow? There were three actions that we could together call a "strategy" in this instance. The first was activating the turn signal, which I did. The second was looking back over my shoulder at the lane, which I also did. The third was looking in the rearview mirror on the driver's side, which was set at an angle so I could see cars that would otherwise be in my blind spot. *That's* what I didn't do—that was the big mistake.

3. Did you make a mistake in execution? After not looking in that mirror, pretty much the entire following sequence was one big mistake in execution. I swerved unexpectedly to the right, nearly cut off another car, hit the accelerator when I should have hit the brake, and ran my first red light. I also nearly gave a perfectly healthy driving instructor a cardiac arrest he did not ask for. So in short, yes, I made a mistake in execution. I corrected too far to the right, and didn't pay attention to my surroundings well enough.

4. What should you have done differently? This is one question the driving instructor asked me. Obviously, I should have checked the rearview mirror. But I also should have been less extreme in my reaction, which almost caused an accident with another car when I swerved right. Also, I should have covered the brake as enthusiastically as I covered the gas pedal. It was like a cascading effect of bad decisions.

5. Were there any warning signs you missed? The car in the blind spot was a *surprise*, so you couldn't say in this particular incident that there was a specific warning sign. But I did miss looking in that rearview mirror, which would have provided me with a warning. In the spirit of ruthless honesty, were there any misgivings or areas of concern *before* the incident? I suppose you could say a certain lack of confidence might have been one. But mainly, just that darned rearview mirror.

6. Did you make any assumptions that turned out wrong? Of course—I assumed the left lane was safe for me to merge into. I assumed that I was invincible without having to sufficiently check my surroundings.

7. Has making this mistake revealed any blind spots or skills you need to practice more? Absolutely. Working on improving my awareness while driving, mastering my footwork between the brake and gas pedal, controlling the direction of the car in sudden situations, and a whole lot of deep breathing.

8. Did this mistake reveal a character trait—like hubris or inflexibility—that's holding you back? There was a touch of hubris here, as I didn't diligently apply what I was taught because I didn't feel I needed it.

9. How will you do things differently moving forward so this doesn't happen again? Make certain I'm following a deliberate three-point process when getting ready to merge left: signal, look over my shoulder, and check the rearview mirror. I will institute a rule for myself for no lane changes unless that happens. I'll also learn how to control my steering, especially in moments of terror. Furthermore, I think I'll adjust my seat so the brake pedal's easier for my foot to reach.

10. If you saw someone else making a similar mistake, how would you advise them? This is what my instructor said: "Obviously, you need to really be aware of your surroundings—but you also have to monitor and control your emotions. More accidents come from fear and fright than any other emotional factor. That will become easier to manage with more practice, of course. Right now, though, I need to find a patch of grass to faint onto." So, something like that, along with pointing out the exact causes and the steps for correction. This is an important step because sometimes we are more insightful and analytical when we remove ourselves from the situation and view it as an impartial bystander.

These 10 questions, answered with utmost honesty, go a long, long way toward giving you the right frame of mind to learn from your actions—even if you honestly answer no to a couple of them.

Although it's tough to keep your mental defense mechanisms from intervening, try to subdue your thoughts, opinions, and intentions—focus squarely on your actions and nothing else. Try to keep it black and white, yes or no. Don't justify or excuse, just give reasons and causes.

When you're assessing your actions, *own* them. Understand and accept that they were your sole responsibility. This might be painful, because we're generally conditioned to search outside ourselves for blame when something goes wrong. We incriminate others or point the finger at outside factors. But only through owning our actions can we take responsibility and improve them.

Introspection can feel scary, possibly defeating, but the fear lasts only as long as it takes you to ask the question. Answering it will provide you with a clear path to learning from your mistakes.

As one of the great sages of our time, Oprah, once said, "When you lose, don't lose the lesson."

You're going to make lots of mistakes. It's unavoidable. Sometimes in order to find out what does work, you first have to find out what doesn't work. But you have to learn from them and not let them be in vain. Ideally, you only make a mistake once and then you never make it again. You can practice all you want, using deliberate, interleaved, spaced, and problem-based learning—but does it matter if you're not on the right path? Don't let your pride get in the way—if your goal is the best performance possible, you know what you must do.

Prioritize It - obviously!

Even if you think you've got your newfound skill down pat, true mastery requires that you never stop practicing or learning about it. That means consciously setting aside as much time as you can possibly devote to practicing and refining your skill as you go along. This seems unnecessary to mention, but why is it so often that we feel that we don't have the proper amount of time for practice? It's our own fault.

The easiest way to set aside time is—wait for it—to schedule it.

As obvious and slight as that recommendation sounds, it's a tactic we often just forget about. Just give yourself some regularly scheduled time over the course of a few months or more to devote entirely to your skill practice: every Monday night after work, or Wednesday afternoon while the kids are in school, or Saturday morning after you've had breakfast—whatever works. Weekly cadences are good and usually easier to remember, but if you think you can find daily time, that's fine, too.

It's just a poor decision to depend on your willpower and suddenly feeling like practicing to keep you consistent. In fact, that's a losing formula. Use a schedule to impose rigidity to your practicing.

Whatever timing you decide upon, *do not change or cancel it unless absolutely necessary.* Your practice schedule is written in pen, while involving others is written in pencil, if at all. This might be the part that's trickiest. Of course, emergencies will come up, but there's also the prospect of socializing with friends after work instead of rushing home to practice—it's nothing to just cancel your regular session on a moment's notice.

This appointment is time you need to take care of *your* needs, and it only really pays off if you and your friends consider it untouchable. Everyone else can just schedule their time around it. This might sound like an easy step, but you're not just doing it for yourself. You're letting others know about your priorities, and they're hopefully taking your needs to heart.

Seriously—schedule away. Like crazy. Not just your practice session—every last thing that you have to do during the course of your day. Many people book almost three quarters of their week the Sunday before it starts—or even earlier if they're scrupulous about the long view.

Don't be unnecessarily tough on yourself when completing a schedule. Try to be realistic about what you can do in a given timeframe. Be reasonable about how long it takes you to do things and how much time you need for breaks and switching between tasks. The point isn't to force yourself into an overly strenuous discipline about your routine; it's to work your learning time around your needs and capabilities.

At least to start with, try scheduling every last thing you're going to do during the course of the day—breaks, lunch, dinner, TV-watching, even sleep. The following schedule assumes that you only have free time after work.

5:00 pm – Commute home/read online news

6:00 pm – Dinner

7:00 pm – Read stories to kids before bedtime

7:15 pm – Decompress/shower time

7:45 pm – Practice with pottery wheel

9:00 pm – Clean up self after pottery wheel

9:15 pm – Check personal email

9:30 pm – Watch television

10:30 pm – Sleep

Reading this aloud might be the pinnacle of mundanity. But especially in the early stages of your learning a skill it can be extremely powerful. Consistency is the primary point of this exercise. It sets up and reinforces the rhythm of your day, making your skill practice an expected, integral component of your schedule, as important as eating, sleeping, and watching *The Bachelor*. It's a great way to instill self-discipline and responsibility as well.

Practice in short bursts. One of the most popular scheduling strategies is the Pomodoro technique. It gets its name from a kitchen timer that looks like a tomato, which is what the technique's inventor, entrepreneur Francesco Cirillo, used to put it into practice. You can use any similar timing device, including a couple online apps directly fashioned after the Pomodoro technique.

It works like this. Set a timer, clock, or stopwatch for 25 minutes. Once it starts, practice (or work) intensely for those 25 minutes. When the timer expires, get up and take a five-minute break to stretch, relax, check the web, or take a quick walk. Then return to your work spot, set the timer for 25 minutes again, and repeat. After finishing four Pomodoro cycles, take a longer break of 15 to 30 minutes for a more extensive recharge. Then start again.

The Pomodoro technique is effective because it channels total focus and concentration over a relatively short amount of time—and you'll be amazed how much you get done after going through a few of these half-hour units, even if it's just a couple of times a day. It's just long enough to accomplish plenty but short enough to keep laser focus throughout. The break time that the Pomodoro technique requires is as necessary for productivity as the intensely focused work time.

Takeaways:

- Now that you understand the foundations of what makes up rapid skill acquisition, the time has come for you to do something about it: practice. But not just normal practice, which is typically a mixture of passive review and regurgitation. True practice is difficult, tedious, and painful. The more you struggle, the more you learn. Keep that in mind.

- There are a few different ways to plan your practice. The first is to use deliberate practice, which involves breaking skills down, isolating trouble areas, then drilling them mercilessly in an attempt to improve overall performance. Take it slow, be patient, and build the right habits and muscle memory from the ground up. Breaking bad habits or incorrect knowledge is far more effort.

- Interleaved practice is a proven idea that seems counterintuitive. Using large blocks of time for learning one topic is less effective than splitting the same block of time into multiple topics—AAA becomes ABC. This helps you connect unrelated topics to each other and keeps you further engaged by not letting you become complacent in your practice. Here, frequency is the important factor.

• Spaced repetition is another kind of practice to use. It is again the notion that what the brain prefers is frequency rather than overall duration. Arrange your study and rehearsal sessions accordingly. Instead of practicing for five hours on Monday, spread it out over the next five days, and you will spend far less time than five hours overall, yet you will retain more. Imagine that a path must be worn in the brain, which can only occur through a sufficient amount of repetitions.

• Problem-based learning is where you deliberately choose a problem to solve, or a goal to achieve, which will necessitate the learning of a skill. In essence, instead of setting out to learn X, the idea is to set a goal of solving problem Y, and in the process, learn X. This will keep you engaged and motivated, and also drive deeper learning because you will take ownership of something and put all the pieces together yourself. For instance, you will need to know what you know, what you don't know, identify solutions, and take action.

- All the practice in the world won't do you any good if you aren't doing it correctly This is where self-assessment, gaining self-awareness, and learning from your mistakes comes in. It requires brutal honesty, trying to view your blind spots, and going through an assessment of questions that force you to answer, in detail, what you did wrong, and what must be changed going forward. This step cannot be ignored.

- An underrated aspect of practice is making time for it. To do so, you simply have to get into the habit of scheduling your practice, rather than practicing when the mood happens to strike you. Schedule your entire day, as consistency is important, especially in earlier stages of learning.

Chapter 4. Deep Comprehension

At this point in the book, you might feel that learning, skills or otherwise, is fairly straightforward. However, at this point, I would regretfully inform you that that's a both true and false statement.

Yes, learning by itself is not a complex matter. Somehow throughout the years, mankind learned that they could drink the milk from a cow, and from many other animals. That was through a weird process of trial and error and imaginative experimentation. Learning is something that can happen by itself, if given enough time.

But that's not the route we want to take. If we want to accelerate learning and harness rapid skill acquisition, then learning requires deeper work. Last chapter, we talked about practice in its many shapes and forms. This chapter is more focused on understanding and comprehension.

It's the difference between trying to milk every animal you come across, udders or not, and understanding what causes milk production and what kind of animals you should be looking for. Practice is something that can make you an expert in the present moment, but knowing how to interact with information and skills, and understand what you're doing and why, is what will set you up for the future.

The first step toward this is something you may have done without knowing. It's called *elaborative interrogation*, which is a fancy term for self-explanation.

Elaborative Interrogation

It sounds intimidating and complex, but it is an easy way to organize and comprehend whatever is in front of you.

It is an important piece of the comprehension puzzle because often, we have blind spots. Blind spots are when we don't realize what we don't know. We discussed them briefly in the prior chapter when we want to evaluate our performance. There, we found them by using strategic questions. Elaborative interrogation simply makes you talk out loud.

It's easily illustrated if you've ever been around small children. If you have, you may have witnessed a phenomenon we call "the why chain." This is when kids ask an initial question about the world—say, "Where does rain come from?"—and, after hearing our answer ("From clouds"), continue down a path of relentless questions to get at a definitive, ending answer ("Why don't the clouds hold in the rain?" "Why can't the clouds just fall to the earth still shaped like clouds?" "Why don't the clouds on a sunny day let rain go?").

This line of questioning can be a recipe for tedium. But you might find that after a few rounds of this, you'll have to devolve your explanation into "Because I said so!" or "Well, that's a good question and I have no idea how to answer it." You just reach a point where you lack a fundamental understanding, even though you can explain it on a surface level.

Through answering that series of questions, you would find out exactly where your comprehension ended (a blind spot for our purposes) and can seek to rectify that if you wish. Congratulations, you've just performed elaborative interrogation.

Simply put, it is an effort to create explanations for *why* stated facts are true. Use a childlike sense of inquiry. At what point can you not provide a credible explanation or answer? This allows you to clearly see what you do *not* comprehend, so you can complete the picture with what you do.

In elaborative interrogation, the learner (you) creates questions as if working through a task. They inquire how and why certain objects work. Nothing is safe from this inquiry. They go through their study materials to determine the answers and try to find connections between all the ideas they're learning about. The answers the student gives form the basis for the next round of questioning, just like the "why chain" that a child might use.

"Why" questions are more significant than "what" questions. "What" can usually be answered in a concrete manner and doesn't require as much understanding. A line of "why" and "how" questions forces you to have a better understanding of the factors and reasons for a given subject. We can memorize all the parts of a flower—the petal, the stamen, the pistil, the receptacle, and so on—but the names alone mean nothing to us. We have to ask what each part of a flower does and *why* that role is integral to its lifespan. Then, we can ask *how* those structures all work with each other to drive reproduction and the like.

This applies to information and topics just as well as physical skills. After all, it's better to know why you must throw a baseball in a certain manner, as opposed to just doing it.

Remember, this method is about exploring what you *don't* know and discovering your blind spots. You wouldn't be able to do this to a topic or skill you don't realize, because you would be stopped after two questions.

"How do phones work?"

"Um..."

Here's an example of using it to clarify your comprehension of a familiar topic so you can go deeper and gain better mastery. Suppose you are learning about the Great Depression of the 1930s. You want to test how deep your knowledge runs and what you *don't* know about it.

- The first thing you'd ask would be, well, **what was it?** It was the biggest worldwide economic breakdown in the history of the industrialized world. It caused a decade of despair.

- ***What caused the Great Depression?*** A few key events, like the stock market crash of October 1929, the failure of over 9,000 banks, declines in consumer spending, high tax on imports from Europe, and drought conditions in the agricultural sector. To name a few!

• Let's talk about the stock market crash in particular. ***Why did it happen?*** Some experts were concerned about margin-selling, declines in the British stock market, out-of-control speculation, and some questionable business practices in the steel industry. These are some blanket causes, so we should dive into one in particular to test the understanding.

• ***Margin-selling? What was that? How did margin-selling work, and why was it a problem?*** Margin-selling (or margin-trading) is when an investor borrows money from a broker to buy stock. So many investors used it that most stock purchases were bought with this borrowed money. It worked so well that the stock prices went up—and when the asset bubble popped, prices fell off. Since the investor had no funds to repay the loan, both the broker and the investor had no profit to show for it. Okay, so this question feels complete. What about the other causes for the stock market crash that were mentioned?

- ***What about the British stock market?* Why did that impact the United States so much? How did it decline so rapidly?**

- *And so on...*

The chain of interrogation goes on from there. There isn't a certain ending point, because it can become a rabbit hole from which you never return. If you can answer something, answer it! If not, make a note that you need to shore up your understanding. Repeat the process and go deeper.

Remember that the overall point of elaborative interrogation is to make sure there are no holes in your understanding. If you can survive your own questioning, it's likely you can survive tests, exams, and other people asking you to teach them. You can start with the journalistic questions (who, what, where, when, why, how), then move onto contextual questions (how did this happen, what happens after, what are the implications) for a thorough start.

The range of topics for which you can use elaborative interrogation is practically limitless. For example, math students can use it to break down advanced calculations and establish patterns that might help in higher-level math topics. If you're studying human biology, you can use the technique to determine the specific conditions that lead to medical conditions like high cholesterol or heart arrhythmia. Even students of literature can use the technique to study motifs, trends, and themes in a particular author's work. You can break down all the aspects of violin technique, such as why you must hold the bow a certain way, the role of rosin, and the role of different types of wood in different tones.

You should be able to see how this lets you know where you lack comprehension and facts. Having knowledge is of course important to learning, but sometimes not having blind spots is just as important.

The Feynman Technique

Elaborative interrogation is just one method of asking yourself questions that focuses on you seeing the whole picture behind a piece of information.

The Feynman Technique, named for famous physicist Richard Feynman, is another way of discussing with yourself. The Feynman Technique is a mental model that was coined by Nobel-prize winning physicist Richard Feynman. Known as the "Great Explainer," Feynman was revered for his ability to clearly illustrate dense topics like quantum physics for virtually anybody. In "Feynman's Lost Lecture: The Motion of Planets Around the Sun," David Goodstein writes that Feynman prided himself on being able to explain the most complex ideas in the simplest terms. It stemmed from his own study techniques as a student at Princeton University, and he refined the method as a professor and teacher of physics.

This method also allows you to gauge your comprehension of a given subject. Properly carried out, the Feynman technique will prove whether you really understand a topic or have glossed over certain important concepts. It's also suitable for almost every conceivable subject, allowing you to see the gaps in your knowledge that need to be connected.

It's even simpler than the "why chain" utilized by children.

The Feynman technique helps to see what you are *unable* to answer—that is the information it provides. All you need to do is honestly answer the questions you are asking yourself, and you will quickly see where you need to focus your attention. It has four steps.

Step One: Choose your concept.

The Feynman technique is widely applicable, so let's choose one we can use throughout this section: *gravity*. Suppose that we want to either understand the basics about gravity or explain it to someone else. Or, we want to see what level of understanding we have about gravity.

Step Two: Write down an explanation of the concept in plain English.

Can you do it? The simpler and shorter the explanation, the harder this is to do. This is the truly important step because it will show exactly what you do and do not understand about the concept of gravity. If you can boil information or a topic down to two sentences in a way that a five-year-old would understand, you probably have a level of mastery over it. If not, you've just found a chink in your armor.

So going back to the concept we are using, how would you define gravity? Would it be something about being attracted to large masses? Would it be something that makes us fall? Or would it be about how our planet was formed? Can you do it, or will you resort to saying, "Well, you know … it's gravity!"

You might be able to explain what happens to objects that are subject to gravity *and* what happens when there is zero gravity. You might also be able to explain the causes of gravity. But everything that happens in between might be something you assume you know but continually skip learning about.

Where does your explanation start to fall apart? If you can't perform this step, clearly you don't know as much about it as you thought, and you would be terrible at explaining it to someone else. The same goes for if your explanations are long, rambling, and deflective. Coincidentally, this is why teaching a skill or information to others is such a powerful tool for your own learning. It forces you to re-examine what you know, and package it all in a way that someone else would have a complete understanding as well.

Step Three: Find your blind spots.

If you were unable to come up with a short description of gravity in the previous step, then it's clear you have large gaps in your knowledge. This step implores you to research gravity and learn enough to be able to describe it in a simple way. You might come up with something like, "The force that causes larger objects to attract smaller objects because of their weight and mass." Whatever you are unable to explain, this is a blind spot you must rectify.

Being able to analyze information and break it down in a simple way demonstrates knowledge and understanding. If you can't summarize it in one sentence, or at least in a brief and concise manner, you still have blind spots you need to learn about. This is a non-negotiable aspect of the technique.

I encourage you to take a second and try this right now. What seemingly simple concept can you try to explain? Can you actually do it, or does it reveal a lack of understanding somewhere in the process?

For instance, why is the sky blue? How television remotes work? How does lightning work? What are clouds made out of? What is digestion? These might be questions you can answer on a surface level, but then what?

Step Four: Use an analogy.

Finally, create an analogy for the concept. What is the purpose of this step? It's an extension of step three. Making analogies between concepts requires a deep understanding of the main traits and characteristics of each, and you can even transfer that understanding into different contexts. You can look at it as the true test of your understanding and whether you still possess blind spots in your knowledge.

What would an analogy for gravity be? Gravity is like when you put your foot into a puddle, and the leaves on the surface of the water are attracted to it because of an invisible attraction to the mass of your foot. That attraction is gravity.

This step also connects new information to old information and lets you piggyback off a working mental model to understand or explain in greater depth. Of course, it's unlikely that you can do step four if you can't do step two and three, but sometimes you can do steps two and three and find you can't do step four. Now you understand the boundaries of your knowledge and better.

The Feynman technique is a rapid way to discover what you know versus what you think you know, and it allows you to solidify your knowledge base. When you keep explaining and simplifying to yourself and discover that you can't, you've just discovered that you don't know as much as you thought you did.

Bloom's Taxonomy

Next, we come to another tool that is useful for gauging your comprehension of a subject or skill, and then providing a guideline for how to deepen that comprehension.

It is called Bloom's taxonomy and it was created by Benjamin Bloom in 1956 (though updated in 2001) as a way to measure the academic performance of college students. It has since been a staple in academic institutions to be a framework for crafting lessons that ensure a thorough comprehension in students. For our purposes, it will help us interact with information better and more actively.

It essentially states that for the highest level of skill acquisition and subject understanding, there are six levels we must be able to complete. Again, you can see the common theme of this chapter of understanding what you need to go forward by isolating what you don't know or cannot do. Most people will never make it through all the levels in the taxonomy, so don't let yourself fall victim to that fate.

The current taxonomy's levels are, from lowest level to highest level of understanding:

- Remember. Retrieving, recognizing, and recalling relevant knowledge from long-term memory.

- Understand. Constructing meaning from oral, written, and graphic messages through interpreting, exemplifying, classifying, summarizing, inferring, comparing, and explaining.
- Apply. Carrying out or using a procedure for executing, or implementing.
- Analyze. Breaking material into constituent parts, determining how the parts relate to one another and to an overall structure or purpose through differentiating, organizing, and attributing.
- Evaluate. Making judgments based on criteria and standards through checking and critiquing.
- Create. Putting elements together to form a coherent or functional whole; reorganizing elements into a new pattern or structure through generating, planning, or producing.

Once you hit the top level of "create" then you can be considered to have a deep grasp on a subject of skill. Without advancing through each level of the taxonomy, you can't adequately perform the next levels. We see this illustrated in our lives every day whenever someone who doesn't have an adequate understanding of a topic seeks to evaluate it and make a judgment upon it. That's because of a failure to follow the taxonomy!

The entire taxonomy is predicated on the mental process of learning, which can actually be summed up quite nicely.

Before you can *understand* a concept, you must *remember* it. To *apply* a concept you must first *understand* it. In order to *evaluate* a process, you must have *analyzed* it. To *create* an accurate conclusion, you must have completed a thorough *evaluation*. The challenge is introspection and understanding where you currently fall on the taxonomy, because only then can you understand what is required for you to move forward in your mastery.

To do that, we will go through each of the levels of the taxonomy and illustrate with an example of learning American history to see how you can learn and acquire more rapidly than before. You'll see that it is a series of questions like other techniques in this chapter. An underrated aspect of skill or topic mastery is thinking about your thinking, otherwise known as *metacognition*. It's nearly impossible to evaluate our own thoughts except through using questions and seeing if you conform to some objective standard.

Remember. This is the very basic stage and the easiest to achieve. It involves memorization of facts. It calls for recognition and recall. It is achieved through exposure to new information and repetition.

Remembering is fundamental to learning. It is critical to remember facts, concepts, and principles for later evaluation and application. If you simply aren't that familiar with prior information or skills, then your understanding will be shaky at best. Without this core concept, you are building your knowledge base on a house of cards.

If you want to learn about American history, you have to have committed at least some aspects to memory, otherwise you will continually lack understanding of events in the greater context. There was a linear sequence of events, and if you don't at least know that, then there is no logical flow. It would also help to know the seminal figures in American history such as Benjamin Franklin and George Washington, and what events they participated in.

This is the bare minimum for understanding because it gives you a clear view of the landscape that is needed. You can't understand while missing crucial information.

Understand. Understanding is much deeper than remembering. Understanding involves having the ability to interpret what the facts mean yourself. It involves asking yourself how the information fit with previous knowledge and the implications thereof.

This phase of the taxonomy speaks to earlier part of this chapter, where you can ask yourself "why" and "how" questions to see how everything fits together. Why did the American revolution occur, and what was the motivation behind it? What was the actual moment that American history began? What was America before it was America? Why, why, why? You can partake in elaborative interrogation in this stage to make sure you don't have any blind spots.

Most people, on most topics or skills, never fulfil this point. They never gain a full understanding of what they want, and sometimes attempt to charge ahead to the next levels of the taxonomy. You can imagine that this can cause some problems later on.

Apply. Being able to apply the concepts learned and putting them into practice is the hallmark of thorough understanding.

Execution involves having enough depth of comprehension of the subject matter and being able to apply it to new contexts, situations, and variables. It requires being able to understand the main elements of the American revolution, for instance, and understand how they might correspond to the French revolution. What lessons for an individual, revolutionary, or fledgling government might the American revolution teach?

The process of application solidifies learning. Instead of learning about how a hammer works, you get to wield it. You get to engage with the subject matter and gain a first-hand experience while seeing how your knowledge holds up while being applied.

Analyze. This involves being able to draw new insights from old concepts, organize ideas, and infer causation.

This fourth stage in Bloom's Taxonomy is the synthesis of the first three stages as, after remembering concepts and principles, understanding them, and applying their learning in real-world scenarios, you are now provided with an avenue to reflect on what went well, what went wrong, and to analyze the lessons learned as a whole.

At this stage, use critical thinking to examine the concepts and principles previously taught. Critical thinking is the proposition that what you see is never what you get—there are always hidden forces in action, sometimes extending far more than you would think possible. For example, how does the American revolution compare to the revolution of other countries? What might have been a better course of action in some instances, and what actions did the British take that failed miserably? What would have happened if the British didn't choose to enforce quartering of soldiers? Why did the colonists feel that the Boston Tea Party would have been impactful? Imagine that you want to gain insight to the inner dialogue of the people committing each act.

At this stage, you scrutinize ideas and figure out what happened, what could have happened, and what should have happened. You analyze the pros and cons of each action, and the implications arising from them. Your focus is on digging as deep as possible, with the knowledge that the actual event at hand is only a fraction of what's important—it's what led to it, and what it caused.

With most information and even skills, most people are only focused on the facts or on the performance. Unfortunately, this might reflect the state of traditional education systems and how detrimental they are to critical thinking.

Evaluate. You now have enough understanding of the subject matter to make an assessment of the ideas learned. Now, you critique ideas and appraise the value of the concepts and principles you know. As mentioned, people like to skip to this step, and thus ill-formed opinions and arguments are born. You probably hear or read these every day, so there's no need to provide an example.

If you have performed your due diligence, you are the proverbial food or movie critic, supposedly a master of the field, and thus possessing opinions that are worthwhile.

In this stage, you too can a credible argument as to the judgments of some of the founding fathers of America. You can argue what was a smart course of action and what was not. You can create your own recommendations for how to handle certain situations, for instance, why the colonists should have begun the fight earlier or later.

Create. Here, you demonstrate such a thorough comprehension of the subject matter that you can integrate these new concepts with previous knowledge and come up with brand new ideas which can be used to solve another set of problems.

How might your knowledge of the American revolution apply to currently oppressed societies? What tipping points exist, what parallels are plain to see, and what do you predict will occur?

By answering those questions, you can create a hypothetical plan of action for those countries that is rooted in history. This stage demonstrates a complete mastery because you can manipulate actions and intentions and insert them into altogether new contexts and issues. You have mastered the lessons and can even modify them yourself now.

Remember that the purpose of Bloom's taxonomy is as a personal barometer. Where do you currently fall in the taxonomy in regard to your desired topic or skill? Have you skipped stages or failed to fully complete some? Are you attempting to evaluate or create when you haven't performed any critical thinking of analysis? You could very well discover what's holding you back.

The Curiosity Muscle

Once again, you have probably come to the conclusion that this learning business isn't as easy as it seems. In the prior chapter, you learned about what practice should really consist of, and here it seems you have just been learning about methods to tediously torture yourself.

Remember, the harder it is, the more you're learning. But it's tough to motivate yourself, even when you know the optimal course of action.

That's why it's time to tap into something that we sometimes forget: we learn because we're curious. At least, learning is easier when we're curious, and we can seek to rediscover our curiosity in the midst of all this practice and self-interrogation we have to perform. Arguably, curiosity is the most powerful tool we have in learning. It's what drives kids to do some of the most dangerous things in the world, and it's also what drives some of our greatest innovations and inventions as a species.

For optimized learning as deep as you want it to be, you need to develop (or redevelop) your curiosity muscle.

All human knowledge—from discovering fire and the wheel to the theory of relativity—sprang from someone being curious. It came from a drive to know more about the nature of the world. Curiosity drives one to dive deeply into the nuts and bolts until they come to a solid comprehension about a subject or situation. And when they get to that point, they're eager to learn *more*. It's a self-perpetuating trait; the more you have of it, the more you want it.

Curiosity begets learning. Every field of thought or skill, without a single exception, is easier to learn if you keep your curiosity front and forward. It's how you can naturally get to the heart of things without feeling like you are working at all.

But curiosity isn't automatic, and it's not something you can just will into existence. Furthermore, some of us are blocked from curiosity because of fear: we tend to have severe anxiety about the unknown, and that anxiety can be particularly high when we're about to *find out* about the unknown.

What we need to do is get more deeply into the nature of curiosity to understand how it really works and how we can use it. Think of this as a preliminary mindset to digging beneath the surface effectively on any topic or skill.

When we say someone is "naturally curious," we usually mean they are motivated by this interest more so than other people. But in reality, there's a lot more to curiosity than simply having a strong desire to know more—people can become curious for quite a few distinctly different reasons. Perhaps the key to better learning and skill acquisition is to find yourself in one of those reasons.

Psychology professor Todd B. Kashdan from George Mason University spent a considerable amount of time researching the nature of human curiosity. Kashdan sought to nail down the diverse characteristics of curiosity into what he called "dimensions."

Kashdan conducted a study with over four hundred participants, each of whom answered three hundred personality questions. Analyzing the data he received, Kashdan developed a model of curiosity that identified *five* dimensions of curiosity. These aspects reveal how certain people are motivated to be curious in the first place. What can help motivate you through the tedium of practice and self-torture?

1. Joyous exploration. When considering the nature of curiosity, this dimension is probably what we think of first: the simple thrill of discovering and experiencing things we don't yet know about. The joyous explorer views new knowledge as a component of personal growth, which for them is its own reward. They're genuinely *excited* about reading all of Shakespeare's plays, trying sushi for the first time, or riding in a cross-country racecar. Amassing a wealth of different experiences and knowledge simply makes them happy.

2. Deprivation sensitivity. This branch of curiosity, on the other hand, is more about anxiety. Someone working from this dimension feels apprehensive or nervous about their lack of information—their being "deprived" of knowledge makes them uneasy. To reduce this pressure, they engage their curiosity. The deprivation sensitivity dimension comes into play when we're trying to solve a problem, getting up to speed with our comprehension, or considering complicated or difficult ideas.

For example, if you're balancing your bank accounts and find you've spent more than you have on record, you get a little nervous, which in turn makes you go through your receipts to see if you've missed anything. If you're taking a philosophy class and the material's going way over your head, you feel anxious about your abilities and study a little harder (if you haven't let fear stop you, that is). When you finally discover or find out the information you're seeking, your discomfort will—theoretically—stop.

3. Stress tolerance. Whereas deprivation sensitivity relates to how uncomfortable one feels about *not* having certain knowledge, the stress tolerance dimension focuses on the uneasy feelings that can come from *getting* that knowledge or taking on a new experience. A person with high stress tolerance in their pursuits is more likely to follow their curiosity. They can just deal with the inherent discomfort of *doing*. On the other hand, someone who can't deal with the uncertainty, disorder, or doubt that arises when exploring new ideas or having new experiences is less likely to let curiosity lead them.

Take two people who have never been on a roller coaster before and are in line to do so at an amusement park. Both of them are at least a little nervous about it because it's a new thing for them. One of them is more willing to confront their fears—they've done so before with other things and have always survived—so they're able to fight through their anxieties and get onboard. The other one, though, lets their fear reduce them into a quivering mass of exposed nerves. They have to take the chicken exit and miss out on the roller coaster.

The first person clearly has a higher ability to tolerate stress, can go past their fears, and will follow their curiosity for a new experience. As for the second person, well, let's hope they *really* like the merry-go-round, because that's pretty much all they can handle.

4. Social curiosity. This dimension of curiosity is simply the desire to know what's going on with other people: what they're thinking, doing, and saying. We indulge this curiosity by interacting with or watching others. We'll have a conversation with a friend because we're interested in a movie they just saw, or we want to hear their opinions on current events, or we just know to hear the latest gossip they've heard.

Social curiosity can also come from a more detached point of observation. A great example of this is people-watching in a crowded place, like a bus stop or Central Park. We might see a couple having a spat, or a couple kids playing a game they just made up, or a man walking his pet duck. (It happens.) Based on what they're doing or saying, we might form certain judgments or opinions about how they really are or how they behave in a more private situation. Curiosity drives us to study them.

5. Thrill-seeking. This aspect is similar to the stress tolerance dimension, except a thrill-seeker doesn't just tolerate risk—they actually *like* it. A thrill-seeker is more than happy to place themselves in harm's way just so they can gain more experience. For them, it's worth the gamble of physical jeopardy, social disavowal, or financial ruin just to have an adventure or encounter something new.

For a thrill-seeking example, look no further than Richard Branson, the hugely successful entrepreneur. He's tried to balloon around the world. He's tried to race a boat across the Atlantic. He's stood valiantly in the path of oncoming storms that destroyed everything else in the immediate vicinity. Branson, in fact, claims to have had *seventy-six* "near-death experiences," including one where he went over the handlebars of the bicycle he was riding. Branson escaped with only minor injuries as he watched his bike go off the edge of a cliff. Clearly, Branson feels extremely comfortable in situations where there's an element of danger. That's your thrill-seeker.

For the joyous explorer and thrill-seeker, curiosity is pretty easy and automatically generated. It's the same for the socially curious, depending on the situation and who surrounds them. For these three dimensions, curiosity is a welcome and comfortable condition. But we may not always feel that way, so we can't really depend on it.

If you're resistant to curiosity, you might serve yourself by considering the origins of your anxiety. If you're feeling awkward about not being "in the know" or left out of the loop, you could use that motivation to drive you to amend that situation (deprivation sensitivity). If you're unable to fight through your fears, you might consider ways to rationalize them and get stronger (stress tolerance).

Curiosity is not a necessary ingredient to your quest for rapid skill acquisition, but it sure makes it easier.

Takeaways:

- Boy, learning isn't a picnic, is it? Practice is tough and taxing, and so is deep understanding and comprehension—the type that truly gives you mastery over a subject or skill. There are a few specific methods to achieve this type of mastery.

- First is known as elaborative interrogation, and you can think of it as a form of self-interrogation, self-summarizing, or self-questioning. You look internally and create an inquiry about a topic or skill. Focus on "why" and "how" questions. Go beneath the surface. Discover where your knowledge ends and begins and discover your blind spots.

- A form of elaborative interrogation is known as the Feynman Technique, which is named for the famous physicist, Richard Feynman. There are four steps to this: choose a topic or skill, summarize or demonstrate it as succinctly as possible, seek out your blind spots through how easy or difficult the previous step was, and then use an analogy. The analogy is considered a high watermark in comprehension because it requires enough knowledge and understanding to be able to manipulate and translate relationships into different contexts.

- Bloom's taxonomy is a method of understanding your level of comprehension. Once you discover your level, there are concrete guidelines about what you need to move to the next level. It consists of the following levels: memorization, understanding, applying, analyzing, evaluating, creating.

- Deep comprehension, despite our best efforts, is often avoided because of the sheer amount of work and tedium involved. Who has the willpower to continually question their thoughts and examine their understanding? It's difficult to say the least. Recapturing your dormant sense of curiosity can be your greatest weapon in learning. It can keep you motivated and in motion when your self-discipline runs out.

Chapter 5. Stack Your Skills

As has been made clear throughout this book, learning a skill is easier than ever before. Because of that, even if you master a certain skill, there's a very good chance someone else has also mastered it. The sword cuts both ways because competition has only increased over the years. If someone were to assess your skills in a particular area with someone else possessing the same skills, they might not see why they should pick *you* to work with over the other person (and vice versa).

Let's consider this an interlude of a chapter because it doesn't necessarily concern *how* to acquire skills and learn, but rather *what* you should focus your efforts on.

It's *not* smart to establish your value or merit on the basis of just one skill. By definition, only 1% of everybody is in the top 1% of anything. (Yes, I double-checked the math.) The top 1% of players in the National Basketball Association is an extremely select fraction of everybody in the league and a *very* small fraction of the world's population. It's almost impossible to get into that 1%. 99% of the NBA comprises players who *aren't* LeBron James or Stephen Curry and aren't doing too badly for themselves. But they are still not the highest paid or most famous players.

In other words, you aren't going to be in the top 1%, so now what?

How do you differentiate yourself from someone with roughly equal amounts of skill and make yourself stand out? Instead of seeking to distinguish yourself based on a statistical improbability, one solution is the concept of *skill stacking*, and believe it or not, it at least partially originated in the comics section of your daily newspaper.

Skill stacking was popularized by Scott Adams, creator of the workplace-themed *Dilbert*, one of the most successful and quotable comic strips in publishing history. The idea behind skill stacking is that, while extreme proficiency in one skill is admirable, it's unlikely; thus it's much more effective to have high abilities in multiple skills which work well together.

Instead of relying on being in the top 1% of a certain skill, shoot instead to be in the top 5–15% in three skills, or even four. It's the difference between imagining you are Mozart, versus being a studio musician who can play four instruments in a pinch. Not everyone can be Mozart, but it's far more likely to be able to play four instruments.

Adams uses himself as a prime example of skill stacking in a career. He realizes that he is not in the top 1% of any skill in particular. *Dilbert*—a comic strip set in an office with amusing "truisms" about the business world—appears in the newspapers in 65 different countries.

Adams reportedly has a net worth of $75 million, the lion's share of it from *Dilbert*, including syndication and merchandise. For a while, almost every office in America had a *Dilbert*-ism on display at somebody's desk just to prove they comprehended workplace irony. So despite Adams not being an extreme outlier in anything in particular, how did this happen?

He's not the most talented comic artist; his characters are largely stick figures with different hairstyles and noses. Let's put him in the top 10% of artistic abilities.

He's not a high-level expert in business and making money. But he did go to business school at the University of California, Berkeley, so let's give him a top 5% here.

He's not necessarily one of the funniest people alive, and has never attempted to be a comedian or anything similar. However, his comic strip is funny and witty enough to be syndicated and have been running for years, so let's give him another top 5% mark on this one.

"When you add in my ordinary business skills," Adams said, "my strong work ethic, my risk tolerance, and my reasonably good sense of humor, I'm fairly unique. And in this case, that uniqueness has commercial value." If you don't believe in Adams as an example, you don't have to look much farther than a 2017 Boston Consulting Group study that found that companies with more diverse skill sets and backgrounds produced 19% more revenue overall.

That's the essence of skill stacking. You simply readjust your goals. Forget relying on being in the top 1%, and instead shoot for getting in the uppermost percentile (5-15%) of a few skills, preferably those that can be used to enhance each other. You leverage the good-to-high skills and traits that you have and combine them in a way to give yourself an advantage over everyone else. Adams blended his above-average business understanding, sense of humor, and artistic abilities, to make a financially viable character that was unique on the comic page. (And Dilbert doesn't even appear to have *eyes*.)

Success is usually considered to be the result of high proficiency in *one* skill, and in certain cases a certain opportunity cost or sacrifice is necessary. Most medical students have to pick one field to specialize in—you won't find a lot of dentists who are also podiatrists. It's the same with sports, where you try to become the top athlete in a specific field like basketball, football, golf, or track at the exclusion of all other sports. Except for extremely rare cases like Deion Sanders and Bo Jackson, you don't find a lot of people who are superstars in two different sports. (Even Michael Jordan couldn't quite hack professional baseball.)

But for almost all other pursuits, high proficiency in a number of skills is much more possible and thus desirable. Skill stacking encourages arranging and using your multiple skills in ways that make you *absolutely unique*—that sets you apart from the others. By combining your ordinary individual skills and learning "gap" skills that you don't yet have, you become a singular person that nobody else can really duplicate. This makes you incredibly valuable in the job market and irreplaceable on a social and personal level.

Skill stacking forces you to look at reality and what really makes an impact. For example, you might be in the top 5% in a certain skill—what will that garner you? You might get a couple of accolades, but otherwise, you won't turn that many heads. At the top of every field resides everyone in the top 5%, so you won't stand out by definition. You could try and push yourself into the top 1%, but if there was a real chance of that you probably wouldn't be reading this book unless you just can't get enough of my exquisite prose.

This means you have to find more ways to be competitive than relying on developing a single skill. Getting into the top 1% of a certain skill is nearly unobtainable (though always worth trying). Being in the top 5% of one skill is great, but once you get into higher levels of a certain skilled population it's not actually that remarkable and you'll be surrounded by similar people.

Therefore, we come again to the conclusion that *more* distinctive is someone who's in the top 10–15% of *three or four* different skills. Having a great specialized talent is one thing—but being very good in a broad spectrum of skills that nobody else quite has? *Now* you've got their attention.

The sweet bonus is that getting into the top 10–15% in a few different areas isn't nearly as hard as getting into the top 1% of just *one* area. The top 1% can take years of practice—that's playing a solo at Carnegie Hall level of skill. However, getting into the top 10–15% doesn't take *too* much more than achieving the goals I talk about in this book: learning, practicing, executing, and repeating. You can probably read a couple of books on the topic and instantly be better informed than 95% of the general population. If you were to read five books on one subject, it is highly doubtful you would learn anything by the time you hit the fourth book, even.

Let's take what's for obvious reasons my favorite example: writing. There are many talented writers. The top 1% will get published no matter what; it's inevitable because of the quality of their work.

Now let's consider the top 5%—they are still flat-out *amazing* writers, but they'll never become popular because they're not quite as good as the top 1%, and they have no other ways to get discovered.

But what if someone in that 5% can also code just a little HTML and knows their way around social media? Not only can this person write flowery phrases, but they can also build themselves a blog featuring their own work, building a brand for them that is personal and unique.

Furthermore, with their knowledge about how to publicize something on social media, they can actually create interest and a global market for their work. And then, *viola*, they actually *get read*. Add into this a certain amount of business savvy, and they will be able to replicate this process to nab more readers, produce more writing, and ultimately skyrocket their revenue from books.

So that writer might only be in the top 5% of all writers, but because they have specialized skills that they've learned in the service of publicizing their work, they've managed to get themselves published and in position to earn readers who become fans—and, theoretically, income. To be perfectly honest, there are probably writers out there who are only in the top *25%* of all writers who are making a good living because they can diversify and build a skill stack.

How Can You Stack Your Skills?

The best thing about a skill stack is that you probably already have one. You just haven't thought about it yet, let alone been able to recognize or discuss it.

The first step in defining your skill stack is making sure you have abilities that work as counterparts and complement each other toward a specific end goal. For example, it's easy to see how writing, public speaking, and acting can create a valid triple threat. Being a competent chef, a smart businessperson, and a capable communicator can be all you need to open a successful restaurant.

Conversely, being a good public speaker, a decent guitarist, and a good chef might only make you a better-than-average waiter—and not bring you toward your desired end goal of owning a restaurant. And being able to type, tap-dance, and shell peanuts effectively—well, some doors may just not be open for you, except maybe circus administration.

The skills you stack can't be too random. They should be three or four skills in related or compatible fields. If you can master those interconnected skill sets, your value could skyrocket far greater than if you just stuck with what you're "naturally" good at doing.

To get to the core of your skill stack, do some relatively simple self-evaluation by asking yourself these questions.

What industry are you in or do you want to be in? Easy enough. What's your current work situation and/or the work situation you dream about?

In that industry, in which areas of skill do people compete against each other? What does everybody in that field of interest absolutely have to do on a basic level? What will get them in the door? These are the skills that the business or endeavor is built on, the ones that the higher-ups will always judge their employees about on a daily basis.

If you're in the top 5% of those skills, it's commendable. But there are still others like you and some who are theoretically *better* than you, so being in the top 5% is not quite enough. Therefore...

Given that everyone has those skills, what new skills can you acquire that will blow them out of the water? This is your "special sauce," the one (or better yet, two or three) additional talents you possess that separate you from everyone else. Chances are, this ability is something you developed in another environment, not specifically for this job or task. And it's the difference-maker that can tilt the scales in your favor. Take a look at the top performers in the field, or in related fields, to get a clue if you're not sure what step to take here.

Let's say you want to be a stockbroker.

In what areas do stockbrokers distinguish themselves from others and compete with each other? Stockbrokers absolutely have to be good at communicating and calculating. That's a given that should cover 100% of all stockbrokers, but let's be more reasonable and say that 75% of them are. Obviously, that's nowhere close to enough to swing hiring decisions your way.

So what new skills can you learn that would separate you from the others? Since the global economy is super-connected, a stockbroker could accentuate their portfolio (pun intended) by learning a foreign language of another economic superpower, like China or Germany. Some studies say 50% of all the world's population is bilingual. That sounds a little high to me, but let's say it's true. You'll distinguish yourself from at least half of the other stockbrokers by being able to speak a different language. And each new language you learn will chip away at that percentile even more. Let's say one language puts you in the top 20% of all stockbrokers.

Furthermore, since biotech is one of the most watched categories on the stock market, a stockbroker with a deeper knowledge of medicine, the human body, and recuperation practice might be a keener analyst of new and prospective technologies. If you know a lot about medicine or have a background in first aid administration or light medical assistance, you could have another advantage over the other bilingual stockbrokers.

You're not a master of all these trades—but with some hard work and practice, it's easy enough to get into the top 10–15%. And that's enough to make you more flexible and marketable to someone else. In this age, versatility is more important than limited execution. You've exponentially multiplied your bankability as a stockbroker just by listening to some audio tapes of German or Chinese every week and reading a few articles a week on breaking news in biotech companies. Not a bad return on investment—and that's just the thing: constructing and increasing your skill stack can be deceptively easy.

Switching to something probably more fun and less stressful, let's consider painting. Close to 100% of all painters (Jackson Pollock-esque, spilling-paint types excepted) have to know how to sketch a given subject. They *all* should need to know how to work with various mediums and paint types, even if they end up specializing in only one or two. For the sake of this example, let's say only 90% of them can work in multiple mediums.

Some only paint portraits or still lifes that are conveniently positioned right in front of them as they paint. But someone who has a well-developed photographic (or at least highly dependable) memory can paint almost anything and anywhere they want, and they might be more prolific in the process. That's a skill that can be honed over time and practice. Finally, someone with a background in mythology, theology, or philosophy might have a grasp on certain symbols that they can incorporate into their work to give it added meaning or tension.

A skilled draftsperson is easy to find among painters. But a skilled draftsperson who works in multiple mediums and has a high-functioning memory and an extremely well-rounded background in art theory, mythology, or philosophy? That's not a common trifecta. And it's easy to use them all in service to art.

Each time you add another skill to your stack, you are creating a more and more selective Venn diagram.

Nobody knows your abilities better than you—but creating a synergy around your diverse skills is something that might have eluded you. Skill stacking can take advantage of what you already are and present it in a way that benefits the masses. And it's also a great, constructive way to figure out what skills you need to learn to make you stand out.

Takeaways:

- A skill stack is something you likely already possess. It's the concept that you can't rely on one skill or proficiency to stand out in whatever you are trying to accomplish. Only 1% of us can be in the top 1% of a skill, and that likely won't be you. Thus, we should create a skill stack that is composed of three or four interrelated skills that you are in the top 10–15% of. It's realistic and will set you apart from your competition.
- A major key is to have the skills be related. This means you shouldn't just focus on your strengths, which oddly enough can hold you back. Take a look at the top performers in your field to see what various skill stacks they possess. When you know what you want to increase your proficiency in, it's as easy as reading a couple of books or a few articles, attending a few lectures, and gaining some basic exposure. This alone will make you better informed and prepared than 90% of the general population—this positions you as an expert!

Chapter 6. Social and Physical Surroundings

An often-overlooked influence on the development of your skills is the general environment that you are surrounded with.

We like to think that our accomplishments are simply a reflection of our true abilities and drive, but frankly that's giving ourselves too much credit. Not to turn this into a nature versus nurture debate, but if someone is born on an island, they are probably going to be a more skilled swimmer than someone who was born without any access to a body of water. You will probably be more knowledgeable about frogs if you grew up in a swamp versus a dessert. We don't get to where we are solely by our own determination.

This comes in two primary forms: the social and physical environments we create for ourselves. Physical environmental factors, of course, include everything in a given space that one can perceive with the five senses—sound, cleanliness, darkness, or light. As it relates to changing your behavior, this could be something that is physically unavoidable or completely absent—*out of sight, out of mind*. Social factors include everything from the people you surround yourself with, customs, and traditions to communication style, support models, and behavior.

The social environment is the people you surround yourself with. They can be the ones who help you advance across the finish line, or they can be the ones who keep you stuck in place by sapping your drive. They can guide you and cheer you on, or be absolutely indifferent. Though it may feel odd to think of people as anchors or balloons, they have the ability to help you with your skills and learning, or drag you down.

For better or worse, our social environment is with us day and night.

A recent study by the *New England Journal of Medicine* closely analyzed a social network consisting of 12,067 people. They had been monitored for 32 years between 1971 and 2003. Investigators had detailed information on the connections: who were friends, who were spouses, siblings, neighbors, and so forth. They also tracked how much each person in the network weighed at specific times over those three decades.

They found that members of this network tended to gain weight when their friends did, increasing their chances of obesity by 57%. This wasn't the case when family members' weights changed; mainly friends and the people they interacted with the most. Whether these friends were located close by or across the country, they maintained the same influence. Very close friends were even likelier to gain weight—if one part of a pair of friends became obese, the other one's chances of becoming obese increased by a whopping 171%.

Whether they think they do or not, those around us have a huge influence on our lives. They can support us, discourage us, or remain wholly apathetic to our goals. Any of these can have a lasting effect on whether we are able to reach our definition of success. For instance, say you wanted to learn piano, but three of your close friends announced that piano was for *nerds* and *losers*. How likely is it that you will persist in this goal, knowing the social pressures and stigmas associated with it? We tend to take others' behaviors around us somewhat personally, as a reflection of our friendship.

When you look around your current social circles, you may not like what you see in terms of support and challenge. But you have a huge degree of control as to what your social circles look like—you just have to learn what to look for and what to avoid. It's not a matter of reducing people to who is useful or who blindly supports you; it's about finding people that provide an atmosphere that makes you want to continue bettering yourself.

The first step, however, is about decluttering the negative.

No Negative Nancys

Whether they're aware of it or not, certain people have a real knack for holding other people back. They're the ones who drain your resources, dishearten and depress you, and keep you behind of where you want to be.

So the first step in shaping your social environment is to show such types the door.

If they're not actively preventing you from acting, then they are telling you that you can't, things are impossible, you shouldn't bother, and asking what's the point. When you hear these things enough, it's inevitable that it starts to pervade your own worldview. The more you find yourself in their company, the more their opinions and outlooks on life are seeping into your own.

You may not think they're bothering or affecting you in any way, but trust me, they are. Of course, there is a difference between someone plainly telling you about reality, but the people that do that will still be supportive of your overall goals.

With the habitually negative, it's almost as if they don't want you to succeed out of jealousy. Often, this is the case because human instinct dictates that we support people and cheer them on, right up to the point where they approach or begin to surpass us.

As such, it's important to realize that the vast majority of negativity and lack of support people will send your way is not about your own abilities, but about their own fears and feelings of inadequacy. Almost all expressions of negativity from a given person spring from one of three ingrained fears: being disrespected, being unloved, and feeling dread about bad things that might happen.

These fears work together to form a worldview that's cranky at best and destructive at worst: the world is terrible and people suck. And through your association with them, they're foisting that point of view onto you. Furthermore, if you've attained some level of success or happiness and you show it, they're likely also filled with envy and resentment.

There are plenty of classic scenarios of people discouraging others based on their own fears.

- The overprotective parent who restricts their child from sports activities because of their own fears of being injured.

- The jealous friend who spews negatively about your relationship because they're terrified of dying alone and unloved.

- The coworker who rants about the office you've been promoted to because they don't feel valued by fellow employees.

When you realize their condemnations and complaints generate from their own unhappiness, it should show you that their misgivings are their own invention—it has nothing to do with you and shouldn't slow you down.

Negative influences are, in their own weird way, opportunistic. If you express an adverse opinion, they'll be happy to back you up, explain why you're right to be cynical or dejected, and give any showing of harmful or negative thinking their full, unqualified support. They'll reinforce your own insecurities and drive you into a well of self-doubt—not a place you want to spend much time. On the contrary, it would be much better if they could steer you toward *empowering* thoughts.

Positive influences try to steer you toward self-belief when you're expressing doubts about yourself—they make sure you can accomplish anything and will try to prove you wrong if you think you can't. They want you to accomplish your goal, and starting with that intention changes their course of action entirely. Negative people, though, will happily serve as an echo chamber for your doubt that drowns out any semblance of hope. Positive people have their foot on the accelerator—negative ones are riding the brakes.

Negative Nancys dwell in their own inaction. They themselves are not happy, but they don't believe they can become happier, and thus don't see any point or payoff in growing as a person. They might not realize they're feeling this way, but they don't want *you* to grow either and will actively try to deter you from maturation, change, and development. They'll cheer you on if they sense you don't have a chance at improving too much, but the moment you come close to success or surpassing them, suddenly they turn into your biggest critics.

An easy question emerges: guilt, obligation, emotional debt, familial ties, sunk costs, and longevity aside, do you want these people in your life? What role are they really serving?

A just-as-simple solution also emerges: limit your contact with Negative Nancys and connect with those who would see you succeed. You have the ability to shape your social environment. Of course, this is easier said than done and may not even be possible—especially if some of the negative people are in your immediate family—but try to arrange things so that you don't have to be around negative people as much as you can.

At the very least, recognize the true message behind other people's negativity and learn to tune it out—because it's not about you at all. You should also introduce some more positive voices to drown them out, as you'll read about shortly.

Role Models, Support Systems, and Hotbeds

Once you've removed as much negativity as possible, the next step is to replace those voices with something more positive. The first part of this is to draw inspiration from others around you that you can observe and analyze. You want to use them as a *role model*.

The idea is to try to use the people around you as role models through observing their behaviors and trying to imagine what their mindsets are. Modeling the practice habits and trying to internalize the discipline of Yo-Yo Ma (generally regarded as the most famous and renowned cellist in history), for instance, would be a good idea for an aspiring cellist.

Whatever your end goal is, someone has already been using the techniques, actions, habits, and mindsets that build the kind of success you're looking for. In a way, you already do this. If you spend any amount of time with certain people or groups, you're quietly adopting how they think and act through osmosis. You even start using the same slang and vocabulary as these people!

The easy part about finding role models is that you don't actually have to meet new people—not yet, anyway. It's all about who you can learn from through deliberate observation. It can start right from the people you see every day that you draw positivity and inspiration from. Just ask yourself—what can you learn from them, and how would they handle challenging situations? Often, the people surrounding us have far more admirable traits than we might realize. This is a way of constructing your virtual social environment before you have to construct the real one.

You can also extend this to public figures, historical figures, and even fictional characters.

Some of the more specific aspects that you'll want to emulate from your model include the following:

External behavior. How does your role model act in relation to other people? What kind of habits, language (verbal and body), and abilities do they display? Study their expressions, take note of their speech, look for little actions that might slip by, and observe how they carry themselves. Close scrutiny of your role model might not only show you how this skilled person behaves, but could also provide clues on how to develop the skill you're trying to obtain. Remember that behaviors and actions are the best indicator of their intentions and what we can best use because they are observable.

With the earlier example of observing Yo-Yo Ma, what is his daily schedule? What does he actually do during practice? How hard does he work and what does he sacrifice? Does he lose sleep over his craft? Does he handle anxiety well?

Internal states and processes. To the best of your abilities, what assumptions can you make about these? What does your role model hold in high value or regard? What kind of emotions, ambitions, ideas, plans, outlooks, and objectives do they support? What drives them and what keeps them going besides willpower? Try to simulate, or at least predict, what their thought processes and reactions are.

Since these are more intangible and less overtly visible than their external behaviors, you might have to make some leaps in opinion about what their attitudes are, but back them up with as much certain evidence as you can get. And just like their external behavior, your model's internal traits could provide hints about how to acquire their skill, or at least how you might approach it. Yo-Yo Ma obviously has self-discipline several orders of magnitude greater than most people, so that's a clear starting point.

Environment. Who is in their social circle? How did they grow up? Who do they see on a daily basis and where do they spend most of their time? How does the environment help or hurt their efforts toward their goals? Take a bigger picture to examine your model's place in the world around them—and how it influences them.

Yo-Yo Ma probably grew up in a strict household and began playing the cello at age four. In fact, both of his parents were also professional musicians. In this instance, it's more important to analyze his environment when he was acquiring his skill, not presently after he is already a master.

The next step up from finding a role model, whether near or far, is to directly find someone that is willing to mentor you. This is where you begin to change your social environment in reality, and there's no better way to do it than to find a shining beacon for you to aspire you. A mentor provides straightforward and personal guidance from someone who's already walked the walk, knows the trials and struggles it entails, and can deliver first-hand advice on getting it yourself.

Ideally, your mentor should be a lot of things.

They should be someone who didn't inherit their success or had it "easy" on the way up. They need to have started from the bottom and methodically worked their way up. You need someone who got their skills through effort, trial, and error.

Your mentor also shouldn't have necessarily been naturally gifted or "blessed." Luck or simple natural talent shouldn't be the main source for their status—those are things you can't teach. Look for someone who had to learn the same things you need to learn and had to apply them consistently and steadily until they'd reached the mountaintop you're looking up at.

Why does this matter? This gives them the ability to break their skill set down to you in the most helpful and purposeful way. People who had to learn from scratch for themselves, without any inherent advantage, understand the exact steps needed for each level and can explain them because they had to do them themselves. On the other hand, people who were naturally gifted and "naturals" often engage in instinctual and automatic behaviors—which aren't so easy to explain or articulate.

In other words, trust a professional basketball player who is 5'8" rather than one who is 7'2" because the shorter one likely had to work much harder and develop deeper skills to overcome inherent disadvantages, while the taller one already possessed the one trait most valuable to basketball—height—and didn't need to learn and develop as much skill. I'm not downplaying professional basketball players who are tall, but there is a reason that a popular saying is "You can't teach height."

A mentor is even more valuable if they have a history of being one to others who became successful themselves. Not only does that speak to their track record, but it also means they probably have an established strategy or plan that you can use for your own apprenticeship—one that's already proven to work for other people. They have advice or a plan that is replicable to some degree, and that's what matters to you.

Good mentors and coaches can quickly spot flaws in your practice and can remedy them before they become habits. They know if you're doing something too much, too little, or incorrectly just by looking at you. There's nothing more harmful than practicing wrong, which is why having a mentor who can immediately repair those errors and tendencies is so crucial.

Quality mentors will always try to test the limits of your skills and nudge you out of your comfort zone. They'll set up challenges for you to master or overcome, but they'll also give you encouragement and emotional motivation to emerge triumphant.

If you can't find an official mentor, then at the very least find a few people you can reach out to frequently, ones you can ask for advice or can talk openly with about your concerns. Consider them your personal board of directors.

As for how to transform the social environment around you every day, an interesting theory is that you're the average of the five people you spend the most time with. They could be all the same kind of people or wildly different from each other, but they have significant influence on your thoughts and deeds.

Is that positive or negative for you and your goals? That's what you have to find out. You never want to be the most superlative positive member—the "smartest," the "prettiest," the "richest"—of any given group, because that means the averages of the other people are dragging you down.

This isn't meant to sound judgmental or catty; it's just that if you truly want to prioritize achieving your goals and expanding in substantial ways, you may need to make some changes to the composition of those five people.

This is likely an uncomfortable process because it involves you seeking out inherently intimidating people. But it's part of the process of improving, developing, and maturing. Don't abandon your friends, your social network, or your groups; just understand the power of your friends on your goals.

The last step, if you can manage it, is to find a group of people who not only exhibit the skills you want to achieve but are driven by them. This is easier said than done. Daniel Coyle, author of *The Talent Code*, encapsulates the benefits of collective skill and artistry in his discussion of "hotbeds of talent."

For example, Coyle mentions the strong concentration of artists that populated Florence, Italy, including Leonardo da Vinci. "Florence was an epicenter for the rise of a powerful social invention called craft guilds," Coyle writes. "Guilds were associations of weavers, painters, goldsmiths, and the like who organized themselves to regulate competition and control quality... What they did best, however, was grow talent. Guilds were built on the apprenticeship system, in which boys around seven years of age were sent to live with masters for fixed terms of five to ten years."

The craft guilds show all the aspects that make for an effective collective: agreement on standards of quality, direct and collateral interest in the success and achievement of all, and a concentration on mentoring others to develop and ingrain skills and good habits. You can imagine the type of raw talent this environment will draw out, even if it is not immediately inherent.

Coyle also talks about soccer players in Brazil, one of the most dominant countries in soccer for decades running. As with the craft guilds of Florence, special attention is given to the development of skills in the form of a specialized, miniature form of the game.

"One illustrative example of deep practice is the 'futsal' game which is very popular among young Brazilian soccer players. The difference of futsal with regular soccer is that the ball has only half of the size of a regular soccer ball, but is twice as heavy. The field is also much smaller. These factors allow a type of deeper practice for regular soccer. A smaller field means greater interaction, less delay and, thus, higher amounts of total training time. The game also demands higher precision of movement. Once the players finally play with a regular ball on a regular field, their skill shines in the virtuosity they are commonly admired for."

These groups are highly unusual because even though they're extremely competitive and intense, there's still a collective goal of mutual improvement. Learning these skills as a group encourages the flow of ideas and examples of how others succeed. For the skill learner, it's access to a lot of valuable information at an immersive scale that can't exist in the "outside world."

The intense, precise focus and the group "mind meld" exist all working hours of the day. It's hard *not* to learn a new skill in such environments. In fact, it's hard not to become an expert after being exposed to such skill on a daily basis so that it becomes your new normal and average. Even the worst Florentine artist of the era, or the worst futsal-focused Brazilian player, is probably far above average for the rest of the world—and that's the power of immersion.

You probably don't have any ties to the era of great Florentine art, and it's only slightly more possible that you're an up-and-coming Brazilian soccer player. But there are plenty of ways to find similar support in a skill you want to develop.

Online sites like meetup.com have international groups devoted to almost any skill you can think of—web coding, painting, blogging, real estate investing, dancing, cooking—and that's just from the top half of their topics page. Many of these groups are further broken down by region, so it's possible for them to meet up personally. These groups are often great sources of knowledge on developing skills, the issues and concerns they bring up, new ideas, techniques, and support for newbies.

The strategies of the Florentine art collective and the Brazilian futsal cooperative are formed around absorptive, tightly focused training. Students worked hard to understand every micro-strategy and nuance of the skill they were trying to learn. To emulate that principle in these modern-day groups requires constant work, open exchange, straightforward feedback, and at least a little competitiveness. To that end, all parties in the group need to agree to follow a high level of focus and an earnest desire to work—anyone just happy to be an amateur won't have a place in this setting. Is this realistic to find? It will be tough, admittedly, but if you look hard enough you can certainly find people seeking out a similarly immersive experience.

Skill acquisition is a personal quest, but nobody does it completely alone. The people who surround and inspire you can help set the tone and agenda for what you want to accomplish (sometimes by showing you what *not* to do). Making yourself open to the right people, and choosing role models and groups wisely, can open unexpected doors, foster new ideas, and help you toward what you want to achieve.

The concept of finding a skill hotbed also segues nicely into the next section on your physical environment.

Physical Surroundings

Arranging your environment to be more conducive to learning is one of the most basic and customizable components of a program to learn new skills. By nurturing your environment to make your self-education more accessible and motivational, you can turn any space into an effective studio where you can concentrate on acquiring, refining, and perfecting your skills.

Just as it's important to encircle yourself with the most supportive people, it's equally significant that you make your personal learning habitat as practical as you need to support your new skill. You probably won't be so lucky as to find a hotbed of learning talent, but we can take practical steps to transform our surroundings.

If you wanted to become a great piano player, how might your environment factor into your improvement? For instance, what if you lived in a piano warehouse? What if you didn't have a piano within driving distance? These are ways your environment can simply make something possible or impossible, much less easier or more likely.

When planning the composition of your learning environment, assume the absolute worst about your own self-discipline.

This is the one point in the entire process of learning a new skill where you must believe or at least *pretend* that you can't be trusted to regulate yourself. You might think you'll be able to break through your laziness, and you might occasionally do so, but this is not something to be depended upon. Your job in this phase is to make your surroundings as foolproof as possible.

Generally, you should design your environment for good decisions. Brian Wansink of Cornell University conducted a study on dietary habits in 2006 and made an interesting discovery. When people switched from serving plates 12 inches in diameter to plates that were 10 inches, they wound up eating 22% *less* food. This finding was so effective that food writers have recycled it as a tip for diet success, to the extent that some espouse using tiny plates and tiny portions to curb appetites.

It's a great example of how even a minor adjustment in an environment can contribute to improved decision-making. The change in plate size was a minuscule two inches—not quite the width of a smartphone—but yielded more than one-fifth of a decrease in consumption. Repeated over time, this minor modification can build up good habits to create major impacts.

This practice is far more adaptable and versatile than you might think. The guiding principle is to make your environment help you learn and make it harder for you to be distracted.

If you want more incentive to practice a musical instrument more, for example, you could make a permanent place for the instrument in the middle of a room with instructions of exactly where to pick up. You could also leave a trail of sheet music that literally requires you to pick it up to walk to your bed. If you want to work out more, you're more likely to visit a gym if it's located on your way home from work, rather than 10 miles in the opposite direction.

You can also put your gym bag in front of your front door, buy a pull-up bar for your kitchen doorway, and only wear shoes that can double as exercise shoes. Finally, if you want to procrastinate less, you can leave reminder Post-its next to door handles and your wallet (things you will have to touch), leave your work in a place you can't avoid it, and hide your distracting temptations.

Decreasing bad habits is a function of *out of sight, out of mind*. For example, supermarkets often place higher-priced items at customers' eye levels to increase the chances they'll buy them. But one could *reverse* this process at home by keeping unhealthy foods away from immediate view and storing them in less visible or harder-to-reach levels. Put your chocolate inside five containers like a Russian nesting doll and put them in a closet—see how often you binge then.

To stop smoking, one might consider removing all the ashtrays from inside the home and place them as far away as possible on the perimeter of their property so smoking will necessitate a brisk walk in the freezing winter. To keep from sitting down all day, you can switch to a standing desk that will force you to stand up during most working hours. You could also simply remove chairs and coffee tables from the area in which you do most of your work.

The whole idea is to eliminate having to make decisions, because that's where we usually hit a snag. Depending on willpower and discipline is risky to say the least, so create an environment that will help you automate your decisions and make learning default choice. More generally, designing for good decisions is encapsulated in two main points.

Keep resources within arm's reach. Nothing derails your effort like not being able to find objects that you need. Sometimes we lose incentive just because a resource is on the other side of the room (not an exaggeration). To correct that, put all the resources you need to learn your skill in immediate proximity to your main workspace. Keep books on the table where you work. Place objects you need in a cabinet that you can reach just by swiveling your chair around. Put your violin on your shoes so you can't avoid it.

Not only will it make accessing these objects more convenient, but it will also help to concentrate your workspace into a relatively compact habitat that should be of great assistance for keeping focus. Make it a game—see if you can have everything at your disposal without having to stand up.

Keep distractions in another room. Pursuant to keeping what you need close by, consider keeping anything that will distract you completely out of eyeshot. You don't have to be absolutely minimalist about what stays in your work area—if that potted plant or that piece of abstract art makes you feel more comfortable, then fine. But if you're too easily lured out of a work session by that dartboard or Nerf gun, physically move them to another room or somewhere in a closet where they'll be out of sight while you're working.

And then, here's the key part—allow yourself to resist the impulse to indulge in your distraction, and turn your attentions to what needs to be learned or practice.

Author Mihaly Csikszentmihalyi, known for the book *Flow*, calls this approach for changing the environment changing the *activation energy* for an activity. Generally, you want to lower the activation energy for a desirable event, and increase the activation energy for an undesirable event. The less activation energy required to start learning and practicing, the better.

Takeaways:

- We like to think of ourselves as being solely responsible for our accomplishments, but it's not true whatsoever. Our social and physical environments have enormous impacts on our thoughts and behaviors every day.

- Your social circle can make or break you. They can be your supporters or they can be negative naysayers. The most dangerous ones, however, are the people who appear to have your best interests in mind but really are projecting their own fears and insecurities onto you. It may not always be possible to break from these people, but at least recognize the source of their criticisms and take them with grains of salt.

- Hopefully you have people around you who you can model—those who function as role models. You may not be privy to their thoughts, so take special interest in their actions and behaviors, because those are the most indicative of their thoughts and intentions. Observe, observe, observe.

• The next step would be finding a mentor—official or unofficial. This is someone who you can bounce ideas off, solicit feedback from, and overall nudge you in the right direction. Ideally, your mentor is someone who has learned from scratch themselves, because they are best positioned to dissect your actions and provide you with useful feedback based on their own experiences and struggles.

• If possible, find yourself a community to immerse yourself in, with the best examples being Brazilian soccer players and Florentine art guilds of the Italian Renaissance. It's difficult, but the idea is to surround yourself with such a high level of skill that it becomes your new normal and average.

• Don't depend on your willpower when you can design your environment to completely bypass having to consciously make a decision. This is where you, generally speaking, keep things around to help you learn and practice, and remove things that prevent you from doing so. It is simple in principle, and leads to the optimal activation energy for learning.

Chapter 7. Manage Your Expectations

Learning a new skill is extraordinarily easy. It's automatic. You just need to snap your fingers and it happens. Thanks for reading. And then the whole world lived happily ever after, achieving everything they ever wanted and eating their favorite foods every night.

The idea that learning in general is easy is an expectation that must be managed immediately. Just about anything is possible—but nothing is easy.

Many times, we grow discouraged and give up because things are harder than we expected, or we felt that we should be moving more quickly. We react to a mistake or disappointing result, and it's tempting to conclude that it's not something we'll ever know how to do. And *that* mistake is more grievous than whatever we did to mess up our efforts.

That's why it's so vital to set reasonable expectations about learning a new skill. It keeps you grounded, and it keeps you striving. There are a plethora of scientific studies that discuss how expectations are a key to motivation. But you probably don't need any further proof than knowing how happy you are when you get surprise ice cream, versus how disappointed you are when you don't get promised ice cream.

If you can pragmatically and accurately envision what you anticipate will happen, your chances of completing inevitably hard work increase. This chapter talks about some of the handicaps that affect expectations, how to work through them, and how to set sensible goals.

Remain Realistic

Most of the time these unrealistic expectations are too optimistic. We have an ideal picture of what we want to accomplish, usually based on seeing a perfect example of it made by someone else. Even though we realistically know that years of practice and work went into that ideal example, if we try to make it just once and fall short we can sometimes feel defeated. It doesn't make a whole lot of sense, but that's often how we think. Imagine how we feel when we watch sports and feel that we could do better in some instances than professional athletes. Unlikely, but a natural thought.

If you have impractical hopes that you'll learn a new skill in a snap, you're going to be beset by disappointment if you lag, fall behind, or miss certain milestones. You'll likely slow down, and eventually you'll get so discouraged that it'll seem futile to continue. After all, the bigger the expectation, the bigger the failure and fall. As this mindset takes hold, it makes it more difficult to finish other projects we have—sometimes, even, with tasks we already know how to do. It also sets up comparisons in our heads that aren't equitable or reasonable, making the whole enterprise seem like wishful thinking on our parts.

Without pragmatic, attainable expectations, the excitement of a new achievement can turn into resentment or despair.

There's no single, universal solution as to what makes for reasonable expectations, and even researchers who study work behavior have differing views. But one researcher at University College London found, after studying the habits of almost 100 people over 12 weeks, that it takes an average of 66 days—just over two months—before a new behavior becomes habitual. Other studies have revealed that it can take around 25–30 hours to conquer the basics of a brand-new skill.

To me, those figures look pretty doable on paper—and yet they *still* may seem like too much time for some. That's perfectly all right. Your main goal is to set expectations that seem reasonable for *your* current situation. Don't sell yourself too short, but don't overestimate yourself either. Don't compare yourself to the achievements of others, because everyone is starting from different natural talents and backgrounds. Just set certain targets that won't fluster you but which are just ambitious enough to create some sense of achievement.

For example, say you want to teach yourself to master French cuisine from scratch. It's easy to come up with too-high expectations in the world of cooking. You won't instinctively know what herbal combinations go in what dishes or in what combinations. You're not going to make a chocolate mousse perfectly. You will not be able to make a certifiably perfect French onion soup within days of practice. In fact, it might take you a few days to even cut onions correctly.

But you can also set expectations that are too *low*. You might just use canned soup for the base of your French onion soup and be done with it. You might just use the same one or two herbs for everything and call it French. Or you could just cheat on the mousse and head straight for the packaged powder you can get in the gelatin aisle. You might not *care*, in other words.

So what are reasonable expectations?

To start out with, at least, realize you're in a learning situation and you don't have to feel pressure to learn everything at once. Learn the basics, and don't assume you can skip steps. Learn how to make broth or stock. Experiment with different herb blends for a while to find out which ones you like. Build skills in beating and folding egg whites or how to make a simple crème fraîche first. And all these expectations assume you already know how to do basic kitchen functions—if you don't, *that's* where you start.

Set expectations according to what you already know, what you *want* to know, and a realistic sense of how much more you'll have to learn to gain the skills you desire.

Don't expect any shortcuts or fortuitous happenings, and simply plan on a slow, plodding, and hopefully linear progression.

A saying among musicians asks, "How does one get to Carnegie Hall?" expecting a pithy answer and a set of directions. The answer is actually, "Years of dedication, hard work, and forsaking all other priorities."

Whatever your goal and whatever path you are traveling, you have to assume that it is the long road. You can't assume there will be any lucky breaks along the way or that you will travel along anything but a linear direction of growth. You can *hope* for it, but planning for it can be one of your biggest downfalls (and disappointments). You just can't anticipate that any shortcuts will magically cut the amount of time you put in and the work you do in half. And relying on them would be an even bigger mistake.

To quote Zig Ziglar, "The elevator to success is out of order, but the stairs are always available." Expect to do the work and expect to reach success after a process. The worst thing that you can feel is an entitlement to success. Even if you have worked hard, nobody is entitled to success—hard work is merely an element of success, not a promise of it.

Refusing to accept the long road also forces you to plan and prepare in a sustainable, progress-driven way.

Let's say that you are about to embark on a 15-mile hike. In the first scenario, you think it'll be a breeze and that you're in great shape already. You don't bother wearing proper socks or shoes, and you only bring one bottle of water. You don't expect to hit any bumps in the road, so to speak, and you don't account for the fact that it looks like there might be a storm on its way.

The temperature drops, it pours for hours, you get soaked, come down with hypothermia, and perish.

In the second scenario, you know that you're in good shape, but a 15-mile hike is far different from an hour in the gym three times a week. You take a couple of practice seven-mile hikes with your boots and a large backpack. You make sure that you have wool socks and broken-in hiking boots, and you bring as much water as your pack allows. You note the weather report and bring a rain jacket and hand warmers.

Which scenario do you think represents better planning by accepting that there's a long road ahead?

If you jump into a car for a 15-minute ride to the grocery store, you might not buckle your seat belt, adjust the mirrors, or take care of your semi-flat tire. You would assume that you can ignore the shortcomings. But you'd act far differently if you were to embark on an eight-hour car ride across the state, because those small actions (or lack thereof) have an annoying habit of compounding.

Everyone in any position of success and glory has expended the requisite amount of sweat, even those that appear to have been born with silver spoons in their mouths. They were fortunate to catch a break, but that doesn't account for their continued success after the fact.

It was American inventor Thomas Edison who legendarily made 1000 attempts to invent the light bulb, and mused, "I didn't fail 1000 times. The light bulb was an invention with 1000 steps."

What's The Toll?

What's your goal with learning? There will always require a commitment of time, effort, and often money. Learning won't ever be free. You may benefit from what you learn in the long run, but there will always be a cost; a sacrifice. This is called an *opportunity cost*, which is what you give up to focus on learning.

You might keep a full and busy social calendar right now, but if you really set yourself to attaining a learning goal, prepare for things to change. You aren't going to be able to continue doing everything you want and nothing you don't. Some of the positives must go, and some negatives must creep in. These are all opportunity costs.

The sacrifices one has to make can be relatively small, like losing some leisure time on the couch, or making more space for your learning in your home. They could also be larger or more severe, such as putting off big expenses to purchase materials you need, taking away time with your family, or changing long-standing habits that get in the way of your new skill. Learning a new skill might also require everyday sacrifices, like blocking out schedule time or scaling down on meals.

There will always be conditions for setting a goal, and you'll always have some need to give something up to get it. The sacrifice need not be permanent, but it must be made.

This is where the ambition ends for a lot of people, because they're not willing to pay the toll that a new opportunity requires. Even if learning will benefit them in the long-term, they're not willing to surrender their present, short-term gratification or comfort to follow through. The thought of even temporary discomfort, let alone *pain*, obliterates their desire to build a new skill.

Most people don't want to let go of any of their present comforts or stable situations. Maybe they're satisfied with what they have and are threatened by the prospect of losing any of it for even a short time.

But when you tally up both sides and weigh the pros and cons, are you really sacrificing that much, or are you just more uncomfortable than you prefer to be?

If you're *not* one of those people, then you already have a clear advantage. You're more than willing to sacrifice or accept change in your ease of life and security to get what you want. And quite frankly, you won't have a lot of competition or obstruction in your quest, because you're one of the very few with the initiative to create something new.

Everything has a toll. Either you pay now by agreeing to sacrifice certain things or you'll pay later by feeling miserable over what you failed to do. You have the time to sacrifice *now*—you won't later.

For example, take two individuals who want to learn how to build a website. I'm going to risk sounding a little out of touch here because there are plenty of easy-to-use applications that can help novices build decent websites with little or no expertise.

One of them decides they want to understand web design as deeply as they can, so he pays a certain amount of money (financial sacrifice) to an online educational site that offers full-length, comprehensive video courses on every aspect of coding you need to become a half-decent web designer. They're very extensive courses, some of them containing up to 300 different "steps" (time sacrifice). Apart from the classes, he feels he needs more hands-on practice to really comprehend the material, so he spends a lot of time on his computer working exclusively on that. He's intent on not being distracted, so he cuts back his time on other Internet sites dramatically (social and leisure sacrifice). This guy's driven.

The other person wants a new website but doesn't want to sacrifice too much in learning time, monetary expense, or social "responsibility" to put one up. He likes seeing his friends four times a week and doesn't want to sacrifice it. Why should he? You can build a website for free at wix.com, anyway. You can't really create your own design or make it look super professional, though. If you want certain levels of service you have to pay a premium, but you can do it for free. And you can have something up in a matter of minutes. After he uploads a few basic pieces and certain formats, there's not much more he can do except add more text and images. Frankly, it's ugly.

Meanwhile, the first person has gained enough expertise after a certain amount of time that he can easily build a very complete, highly functional and attractive website in a fairly short amount of time. And he's used what he learned to make *other* apps, maybe even full-blown programs. His talent is obvious, his work is admired, he's made his monetary investment back, and he gets his own *Bachelor*-type show on a major network. Look at that payoff for his temporary sacrifices.

Okay, so I made up the last part of the story, but the point is clear. The sacrifices the first person was willing to make—and to be honest, they weren't really *huge*—led to a more complete, practiced, and expert human being with skills he didn't have just a short time ago. Whereas the second guy, who I'm sure is a perfectly decent human being, just took the easiest routes possible without sacrificing much of anything. He's produced *something*, but his range is ultimately limited because he can't customize it himself. So he's restricted to what he's allowed to do by a company that's probably run by people like the *first* guy.

Which of these people has completed his journey with the more complete, reliable, and knowledgeable set of skills? You already know the answer to this question. Perhaps this section is a long way to say that you can't have your cake and eat it too.

Constant Confusion

Another important mindset to manage is confusion and frustration. Get comfortable with them.

One of the reasons why learning stops is that people are not looking forward to being in a state of confusion, of not knowing what to do or where to take an idea. It's uncomfortable and decidedly not pleasurable.

And so if you are to have any hope of achieving your goals, you'll need to learn how to persist through the mess and confusion that any worthwhile task necessarily involves. Such persistence is what Michael Gelb, in his book *How to Think Like Leonardo da Vinci,* calls *confusion endurance.*

This concept teaches that in order to achieve, you must have the ability to endure the confusion that comes with the task. This confusion may come as a result of not knowing where to start, being perplexed at how to attack a problem, having a muddied view of what you're trying to achieve, wondering what resources are available and relevant to the task, and the like. This is especially present in learning, where you are often starting from ground zero—frustration city.

Confusion endurance is all about being able to stay with a task and persisting instead of just abandoning it when things get difficult. It's about being able to persevere when you have the uncertainty and confusion of juggling multiple balls and not knowing where they will all land. It's the feeling of coming to a fork in the road with 10 paths and having to analyze each path. Annoying. But also conquerable if you just deal with things one at a time.

Suppose you're standing in the middle of a messy room filled with boxes upon boxes of clutter to move and organize. It's an uncomfortable feeling to be surrounded by essentially chaos. It can cause some to hyperventilate and start sweating at the thought of it.

That's when you come to the fork in the road. If you don't have the ability to endure the chaos created by the mountain of disorganized clutter around you, you'll never stay with the task long enough to figure out a viable solution.

You'll need to have enough confusion endurance to withstand the initial disarray you're faced with, as well as the personal bewilderment you may feel from not knowing where to start or how to get the task done. As you learn to sustain your efforts to categorize, organize, and structure the things around you, you also get closer and closer to the solution you need to finish your goal.

Confusion endurance is about having the stamina to get down to work and keep working through tough times instead of just waiting for inspiration to strike.

You Know Nothing

You know nothing. This is the mindset of putting yourself in the shoes of a perpetual student—in every situation. A student is humble, willing to listen, and open to new information and perspectives.

Adopting a beginner "I know nothing" mindset shouldn't be a blow to the ego, although it sounds like you should devalue yourself in favor of others. What you're doing is not related to your ego—it's just putting yourself in a position to be able to listen to others and keep improving yourself bit by bit. The ego hates to admit it, but imagine how much differently you would act if you could just state with a straight face, "I don't know anything and I'm willing to hear you out and really listen to you." Your chances of continued success run much higher with that mindset than with one that's closed off to learning.

The mindset of a beginner—even to the point of considering yourself a novice or amateur in something you've known about for years—is beneficial in helping you learn.

At least, it's miles better than considering yourself an expert and using the "I know this already" mindset.

A common misconception about being an expert—even among experts—is that it implies you don't have to learn anything anymore. You've reached the fullest extent of knowledge possible in a given situation, and any suggestion that you could still learn more is almost insulting. You think—or feel—that you've already transcended all limitations and that there's nowhere to go but down.

The beginner's mindset is drawn from a Zen Buddhist concept, described as "having an attitude of openness, eagerness, and lack of preconceptions when studying a subject, even when studying at an advanced level, just as a beginner in that subject would."

Every time you come across a new situation, no matter how much you think you know, reorient yourself to experiencing it as a beginner. Release all of your preconceived notions or expectations about the experience. Treat it with the curiosity and sense of wonder as if you were seeing it for the first time.

Let's take an example of learning how to play a new instrument. What questions would you ask? Where would you even start? You wouldn't know what's important, so everything would seem significant at first. You'd probably be curious as to the limits of the instrument—first in how to not break it and then in its overall capabilities. You'd be filled with wonder and also caution in the fear of making an error or breaking it. The impression it makes on you immediately won't be forgotten for a very long time.

Those are the underpinnings of the beginner mindset. When you try to reprogram your mind to a blank slate and act as if you truly have no knowledge about something, knowledge will come far easier than acting like you do through the form of extensive questioning and curiosity. Approaching an instrument as an expert typically makes you skip a few steps, without giving a single thought as to whether you should skip anything.

It should be emphasized that the beginner's mindset empowers the ability to ask *dumb questions*. So-called experts rely on assumptions and their own experiences, often without further investigation. When you feel comfortable asking *dumb questions*, nothing is left up to assumptions and chance, and everything is out in the open and clarified.

Seeing the same information from a different angle might be all you need to break through a plateau or reach an epiphany. That's the real value of the beginner's mindset. Sometimes we are so entrenched in our perspectives that it's impossible to see what we might be missing.

The beginner's mindset requires slowing down and paying attention to what you've ignored for a long time.

Takeaways:

- Setting expectations on how you are able to learn a new skill is important to staying on track and not giving up completely. Too high and you may feel discouraged; too low and you may feel bored and unengaged. Habits have been shown to take over two months to form, and new skills have been shown to take at least 25 hours to become any good at. So don't despair when you aren't naturally skilled and proficient. It's all part of the discomfort of the learning curve.

• Expect that there is a long road ahead of you. Don't rely on or expect shortcuts. To want anything more than a steady, linear progression in learning a new skill is a pipedream. Stay realistic—you know yourself, and don't compare yourself to the standards of anyone else.

• Everything in this world you want represents a sacrifice, though some are not as apparent as others. Learning a new skill certainly will involve numerous sacrifices, be they big or small. This is where the wheat separates itself from the chaff because most people are either unaware or unwilling to make those sacrifices on a daily basis. Nothing is free!

• The last mindset to keep in mind is that wherever you are and whatever your level, you know nothing. Truly. When you can believe that, you approach the entire process of learning differently. Something familiar can still be rediscovered, and something new demands even greater attention and analysis.

Summary Guide

Chapter 1. Learn with Rapid Skill Acquisition

• What is learning? Beyond the pain and discomfort and annoyance, learning represents the ability to change your life and circumstances. The problem is, we were never taught how to learn because most of our schooling tended to be passive. Unfortunately, the skill of regurgitating information and filling in the blanks does not serve us well in the real world. What serves us is knowing the most effective methods for learning a skill.

• An important step in learning is to figure out what you want to learn. We have many desires but should only devote our precious time to things that matter. What matters? Things that can increase our happiness and bankability, capitalize on a strength, enhance a life purpose, make the most of an opportunity, or cope with a life circumstance. Not every skill, hobby, or piece of information is created equally, especially in terms of what will create a shift in your life.

• There are four important stages of learning to familiarize yourself with. When you know where you are, you can plan much better the next steps you need to take. The four stages are *unconscious incompetence* (you don't know what you don't know), *conscious incompetence* (you know what you're doing wrong), *conscious competence* (you know how to succeed, but it takes effort and focus), and *unconscious competence* (you can succeed without thinking about it).

Chapter 2. Strategic Planning

• For optimal learning, plan to deconstruct your skill into smaller subskills. This helps you psychologically as it is easier to face a series of small tasks versus one large task. It also helps you use your time wisely because when you deconstruct, you can figure out which subskills or areas of inquiry have the biggest impact. This is exemplified by the 80/20 Rule—just like in learning languages, where the majority of daily conversations only use a few hundred vocabulary words.

• Be willing to learn and mix styles and mediums of learning. Though the jury is certainly out on the scientific efficacy of stylistic differences, the reality is that learning can only occur when you can pay sufficient attention and maintain adequate focus. That's just harder in some mediums and styles for some people over others. There's no downside to having different types of ammunition for learning. There are two models we talk about: the learning pyramid (reading, listening, doing, teaching, etc.), and the Solomon-Felder index of learning styles (active, passive, global, sequential, etc.).

• The final (or for some, primary) aspect to creating a plan for learning is to understand how to effectively gather information and filter resources. After all, not all sources are created equal. This consists of a few steps involving looking for dissenting information, looking at overall trends and patterns, and constructing a nuanced overview. During this phase, many people get stuck on the information-gathering phase, and it inhibits them from action. Know that you will never know everything, and you must consciously choose to stop learning at some point.

Chapter 3. It's Just Practice

• Now that you understand the foundations of what makes up rapid skill acquisition, the time has come for you to do something about it: practice. But not just normal practice, which is typically a mixture of passive review and regurgitation. True practice is difficult, tedious, and painful. The more you struggle, the more you learn. Keep that in mind.

• There are a few different ways to plan your practice. The first is to use deliberate practice, which involves breaking skills down, isolating trouble areas, then drilling them mercilessly in an attempt to improve overall performance. Take it slow, be patient, and build the right habits and muscle memory from the ground up. Breaking bad habits or incorrect knowledge is far more effort.

• Interleaved practice is a proven idea that seems counterintuitive. Using large blocks of time for learning one topic is less effective than splitting the same block of time into multiple topics—AAA becomes ABC. This helps you connect unrelated topics to each other and keeps you further engaged by not letting you become complacent in your practice. Here, frequency is the important factor.

• Spaced repetition is another kind of practice to use. It is again the notion that what the brain prefers is frequency rather than overall duration. Arrange your study and rehearsal sessions accordingly. Instead of practicing for five hours on Monday, spread it out over the next five days, and you will spend far less time than five hours overall, yet you will retain more. Imagine that a path must be worn in the brain, which can only occur through a sufficient amount of repetitions.

- Problem-based learning is where you deliberately choose a problem to solve, or a goal to achieve, which will necessitate the learning of a skill. In essence, instead of setting out to learn X, the idea is to set a goal of solving problem Y, and in the process, learn X. This will keep you engaged and motivated, and also drive deeper learning because you will take ownership of something and put all the pieces together yourself. For instance, you will need to know what you know, what you don't know, identify solutions, and take action.

- All the practice in the world won't do you any good if you aren't doing it correctly This is where self-assessment, gaining self-awareness, and learning from your mistakes comes in. It requires brutal honesty, trying to view your blind spots, and going through an assessment of questions that force you to answer, in detail, what you did wrong, and what must be changed going forward. This step cannot be ignored.

- An underrated aspect of practice is making time for it. To do so, you simply have to get into the habit of scheduling your practice, rather than practicing when the mood happens to strike you. Schedule your entire day, as consistency is important, especially in earlier stages of learning.

Chapter 4. Deep Comprehension

- Boy, learning isn't a picnic, is it? Practice is tough and taxing, and so is deep understanding and comprehension—the type that truly gives you mastery over a subject or skill. There are a few specific methods to achieve this type of mastery.

- First is known as elaborative interrogation, and you can think of it as a form of self-interrogation, self-summarizing, or self-questioning. You look internally and create an inquiry about a topic or skill. Focus on "why" and "how" questions. Go beneath the surface. Discover where your knowledge ends and begins and discover your blind spots.

- A form of elaborative interrogation is known as the Feynman Technique, which is named for the famous physicist, Richard Feynman. There are four steps to this:

choose a topic or skill, summarize or demonstrate it as succinctly as possible, seek out your blind spots through how easy or difficult the previous step was, and then use an analogy. The analogy is considered a high watermark in comprehension because it requires enough knowledge and understanding to be able to manipulate and translate relationships into different contexts.

• Bloom's taxonomy is a method of understanding your level of comprehension. Once you discover your level, there are concrete guidelines about what you need to move to the next level. It consists of the following levels: memorization, understanding, applying, analyzing, evaluating, creating.

• Deep comprehension, despite our best efforts, is often avoided because of the sheer amount of work and tedium involved. Who has the willpower to continually question their thoughts and examine their understanding? It's difficult to say the least. Recapturing your dormant sense of curiosity can be your greatest weapon in learning. It can keep you motivated and in motion when your self-discipline runs out.

Chapter 5. Stack Your Skills

• A skill stack is something you likely already possess. It's the concept that you can't rely on one skill or proficiency to stand out in whatever you are trying to accomplish. Only 1% of us can be in the top 1% of a skill, and that likely won't be you. Thus, we should create a skill stack that is composed of three or four interrelated skills that you are in the top 10–15% of. It's realistic and will set you apart from your competition.

• A major key is to have the skills be related. This means you shouldn't just focus on your strengths, which oddly enough can hold you back. Take a look at the top performers in your field to see what various skill stacks they possess. When you know what you want to increase your proficiency in, it's as easy as reading a couple of books or a few articles, attending a few lectures, and gaining some basic exposure. This alone will make you better informed and prepared than 90% of the general population—this positions you as an expert!

Chapter 6. Social and Physical Surroundings

• We like to think of ourselves as being solely responsible for our accomplishments, but it's not true whatsoever. Our social and physical environments have enormous impacts on our thoughts and behaviors every day.

• Your social circle can make or break you. They can be your supporters or they can be negative naysayers. The most dangerous ones, however, are the people who appear to have your best interests in mind but really are projecting their own fears and insecurities onto you. It may not always be possible to break from these people, but at least recognize the source of their criticisms and take them with grains of salt.

• Hopefully you have people around you who you can model—those who function as role models. You may not be privy to their thoughts, so take special interest in their actions and behaviors, because those are the most indicative of their thoughts and intentions. Observe, observe, observe.

• The next step would be finding a mentor—official or unofficial. This is someone who you can bounce ideas off, solicit feedback from, and overall nudge you in the right direction. Ideally, your mentor is someone who has learned from scratch themselves, because they are best positioned to dissect your actions and provide you with useful feedback based on their own experiences and struggles.

• If possible, find yourself a community to immerse yourself in, with the best examples being Brazilian soccer players and Florentine art guilds of the Italian Renaissance. It's difficult, but the idea is to surround yourself with such a high level of skill that it becomes your new normal and average.

• Don't depend on your willpower when you can design your environment to completely bypass having to consciously make a decision. This is where you, generally speaking, keep things around to help you learn and practice, and remove things that prevent you from doing so. It is simple in principle, and leads to the optimal activation energy for learning.

Chapter 7. Manage Your Expectations

- Setting expectations on how you are able to learn a new skill is important to staying on track and not giving up completely. Too high and you may feel discouraged; too low and you may feel bored and unengaged. Habits have been shown to take over two months to form, and new skills have been shown to take at least 25 hours to become any good at. So don't despair when you aren't naturally skilled and proficient. It's all part of the discomfort of the learning curve.

- Expect that there is a long road ahead of you. Don't rely on or expect shortcuts. To want anything more than a steady, linear progression in learning a new skill is a pipedream. Stay realistic—you know yourself, and don't compare yourself to the standards of anyone else.

- Everything in this world you want represents a sacrifice, though some are not as apparent as others. Learning a new skill certainly will involve numerous sacrifices, be they big or small. This is where the wheat separates itself from the chaff because most people are either unaware or unwilling to make those sacrifices on a daily basis. Nothing is free!

- The last mindset to keep in mind is that wherever you are and whatever your level, you know nothing. Truly. When you can believe that, you approach the entire process of learning differently. Something familiar can still be rediscovered, and something new demands even greater attention and analysis.

Printed by Amazon Italia Logistica S.r.l.
Torrazza Piemonte (TO), Italy